Asian Democracy in World History

How does the democratic experience in Asia, in countries with unique and totalitarian political traditions, compare with democracies worldwide? Is the aspiration to freedom universal or is it a product of Western ideas and institutions?

Taking a comparative approach, Alan T. Wood traces the evolution of democracy from its origins in prehistoric times, and describes democratic growth in 13 Asian countries from Japan in East Asia to Pakistan in South Asia.

Periods and topics discussed include:

- the background of Western democracy
- post-war democracies in India, Japan, and the Philippines
- later democracies in South Korea, Taiwan, and the prospects for China
- later democracies in Thailand, Malaysia, Singapore, and Indonesia
- fragile democracies in Pakistan, Bangladesh, and Sri Lanka.

Providing suggestions for further reading that include Internet sources, this is an ideal starting point for in-depth study of democracy in the entire Asian region.

Alan T. Wood is Professor of History at the University of Washington, Bothell. He has lived and studied in Asia for many years, and is the author of *Limits to Autocracy: From Sung Neo-Confucianism to a Doctrine of Political Rights* (1995) and *What Does It Mean to be Human? A New Interpretation of Freedom in World History* (2001).

Themes in World History
Series editor: Peter N. Stearns

The *Themes in World History* series offers focused treatment of a range of human experiences and institutions in the world history context. The purpose is to provide serious, if brief, discussions of important topics as additions to textbook coverage and document collections. The treatments will allow students to probe particular facets of the human story in geater depth than textbook coverage allows, and to gain a fuller sense of historians' analytical methods and debates in the process. Each topic is handled over time – allowing discussions of changes and continuities. Each topic is assessed in terms of a range of different societies and religions – allowing comparisons of relevant similarities and differences. Each book in the series helps readers deal with world history in action, evaluating global contexts as they work through some of the key components of human society and human life.

Asian Democracy in World History

Alan T. Wood

Routledge
Taylor & Francis Group

NEW YORK AND LONDON

First published 2004
by Routledge
29 West 35th Street, New York, NY 1001

Simultaneously published in the UK
by Routledge
11 New Fetter Lane, London EC4P 4EE

Routledge is an imprint of the Taylor & Francis Group

© 2004 Alan T. Wood

Typeset in Garamond and Gill Sans by Exe Valley Dataset Ltd, Exeter
Printed and bound in Great Britain by TJ International Ltd, Padstow, Cornwall

Library of Congress Cataloging in Publication Data
Wood, Alan Thomas.
  Asian democracy in world history / Alan T. Wood
    p. cm. – (Themes in world history)
  Includes bibliographical references.
  1. Democracy–Asia. 2. Democracy. 3. World history.
  I. Title. II. Series.
JQ36.W66 2003
321.8′095–dc21   2003010249

British Library Cataloguing in Publication Data
A catalogue record for this book is available from the British Library

ISBN 0–415–22942–1 (hbk)
ISBN 0–415–22943–x (pbk)

To students in Asia and everywhere, whose desire
for freedom and democracy is irrepressible.
May you never give up hope.

Contents

Preface

Many years ago, when I was in college, I remember running across a cartoon in the *New Yorker* that depicted Adam and Eve walking out of the Garden of Eden after having been expelled for eating the forbidden fruit. For understandable reasons, they looked a bit down. Adam turned to his companion and said, with that blinding insight into the obvious that we have all come to associate with the male gender, 'Eve, we live in an age of transition.'

And so we do. To be sure, most historians start out their books claiming that the period they are about to talk about is more important than most people realize. They are usually right. My claim is at once more modest and more ambitious. It is more modest because I am not the first to point out that the institution of democracy is spreading widely throughout the world. It is more ambitious because very few, if any, have situated their subject in the larger context of world history. In this book I will argue that the significance of the spread of democracy to Asia becomes most fully apparent when we adopt a global historical perspective. For the past 500 years, the main theme of world history was the ascendancy of European power over Asia, Africa, and the Americas, driven by rapid improvements in nautical, military, and then industrial technology that were initially confined to Europe.

In the first half of the twentieth century, however, Europeans turned that same technology on themselves in two world wars. The savagery and barbarity unleashed by the Great War (1914–18), followed by the long catalog of human suffering in the Holocaust and the Second World War, undermined the self-confidence of Western culture. The impact of these catastrophes eroded the institutions and conditions of democracy in Europe, destroyed the illusion of progress that the scientific revolution had bequeathed to many Europeans, and ultimately dismantled the European colonial empires and the European dominance of the world economy. The optimism of the nineteenth century turned to despair, from which many Americans and Europeans attempted to distract themselves by mindless consumerism in the 1920s (and some would argue thereafter).[1] The residue from the two world wars, in the form of a Cold War that divided the world into rival camps of democratic and totalitarian states, then hung over world politics like a shroud until the collapse of the Soviet Union in the early 1990s. In some places, such as North Korea, the effects of the Cold War linger on.

We may now have turned a corner. At the beginning of a new millennium, the global community has more grounds for hope than it has had for centuries. The fruits of the industrial revolution are being distributed more equitably around the world (though with many accompanying inequities, as we shall see), and many more people are free to choose their governments than at any time in human history. That hope, however, must be tempered by the awesome challenges ahead of us. Modern technology has now reached a stage where, for the first time, we have the power to destroy our own species on the planet through war, to undermine the viability of life through our poisoning of the environment, or to change human nature itself irrevocably through genetic manipulation. In the past we had the luxury of slaughtering each other or polluting our environment on a local scale. Today we do so on a global scale. War (along with its stepchild terrorism) and environmental degradation thus constitute the greatest challenges to the world today. Everything else pales by comparison.

If we were to confront these challenges with the institutional tools of the early twentieth century – the dictatorial nation-state – we would have little hope of succeeding. Now, however, the success of democracies opens up the possibility of developing new institutions of global cooperation that could reduce the likelihood of war and mitigate the environmental degradation we have thus far precipitated. As a general rule (though there are exceptions) democracies are less inclined to foster war, and more inclined to collaborate with each other, than their authoritarian or totalitarian counterparts. We may, in effect, have just passed through an institutional watershed in human history that offers real hope for the future of humankind. This study is designed to pursue this larger theme through assessing the roots of Asian democracy and its overall sustainability.

My hope is that Western readers may come to understand more deeply how precious democracy is, and how varied its manifestations are in countries with vastly different historical and institutional traditions. If the reader begins to appreciate his or her own democracy more deeply, so much the better. Our own experiment with democracy can flourish only if you and I are willing to participate in it with compassion and responsibility. Above all, this book will try to demonstrate clearly that the desire for freedom is universal. To be human is to be free. To be free, as I shall argue below, is to accept constraints. The self-constraint on which democracy is based is enhanced through education, property, stability, and prosperity; it is diminished through poverty, war, disease, natural disasters, and famine.

Let me add a final word about the content of the book, which has quite deliberately stressed breadth over depth in order to provide the broadest possible comparative perspective. I have also tried whenever possible to reduce to a bare minimum the paraphernalia of academic writing, especially footnotes. At the end of every chapter I have included a list of further readings for those curious readers who may wish to dig more deeply into some of the topics I raise in the text.

The alert reader will note that I have not included many countries, such as Vietnam and Burma, as well as significant regions such as Central Asia (comprised primarily of former Soviet republics) and West Asia (the Middle East). There are two principal reasons. The first is that democracy has not, as yet, been notably successful in those places. One can only hope that a future edition of this book, if there is ever to be one, would be able to include them. The second reason derives from an effort to keep all the books in this series on world history to a modest size.

The work is organized both topically and chronologically. First come two chapters designed to introduce the overall topic of democracy and then trace its origin from hunting and gathering societies to the present in the West. I then cover the three democracies in Asia that emerged after the Second World War: India, Japan, and the Philippines. That is followed by a chapter on the later democracies of East Asia: South Korea and Taiwan. China was included in the book – even though it is not a democracy – because of its strategic significance in world history, and because the future peace and stability of the world depends in part on the ability of the world community to encourage a successful transition to democracy in China. From there the attention shifts to Southeast Asia, where in Thailand, Malaysia, Singapore, and Indonesia significant steps have been taken in the past decade or so to cross the bridge from authoritarian to democratic rule. In Pakistan, Bangladesh, and Sri Lanka, there have been both advances and retreats in the evolution of democratic institutions. In the conclusion I try to answer the question 'so what?'

Throughout the book I emphasize the crucial importance of understanding how the historical and cultural background of each country influences the politics in the present. The benefit of that approach is that it enables the reader to appreciate the unique situation of each nation's experience so that one is less tempted to make generalizations that may apply to one set of cultural circumstances but not to another. Only then can an observer become fully aware of the complexity of the interactions involved in the evolution of human institutions, the impact of the different internal traditions that led to different emphases in modern democratic practice in each country, and the huge historical and contemporary variety of Asia. But there is a drawback to this organizing principle of emphasizing the historical experience of each country as well. It may seem that, to paraphrase Elbert Hubbard's observation about life, the book is just a compendium of 'one damned thing after another.' I have tried to mitigate this outcome as much as possible by stressing parallels when they seem appropriate, and by trying to weave the threads into a more coherent pattern in the final chapter.

One of the many pleasures of writing a book is the chance to communicate with an audience beyond the range of the human voice. E-mail now makes that easier than ever before. I would be delighted to hear your reactions and comments – including those pointing out errors of fact or differences of interpretation – as well as suggestions for improvement. I can be reached at awood@u.washington.edu.

1 For a global treatment of this phenomenon, see Peter N. Stearns, *Consumerism in World History: The Global Transformation of Desire* (London and New York: Routledge, 2001).

Acknowledgments

I would like to express my gratitude to the students over the years whose perspective, and probing questions, have always added new understanding to the subject: Bill Abbott, Eric Alm, Woo-chul Chung, Julette Cotter, Vey Damneun, Charlie Fielden, Gena Lupo, Jennifer McDonough, and Jingwei Zhong. My colleague at the University of Washington, Bothell, Constantin Behler, has applied his formidable intellect to the early chapters and offered many helpful suggestions. Stephen Goodlad has given me the benefit of his scholarly understanding of democracy, as well has his vast editorial skills, to improve the manuscript significantly. Neither agrees with all my assertions, and it goes without saying that none of the folks mentioned here should be held accountable for errors of either fact or interpretation, for which I alone bear responsibility. From the students and faculty with whom we sailed on two voyages around the world on the Semester at Sea program, in the fall of 1993 and the spring of 2000, I have learned more about democracy than they can possibly imagine. My daughter Irene, my son Brian, and his wife Iman Issa never fail to delight with their imaginative interpretations of the world around them. My wife Wei-ping began her own odyssey as a first-year law student while this manuscript was in its final stages, and yet still managed to provide unfailing support for the whole enterprise. How she does so many things, so well, I will never know, and I can never thank her enough.

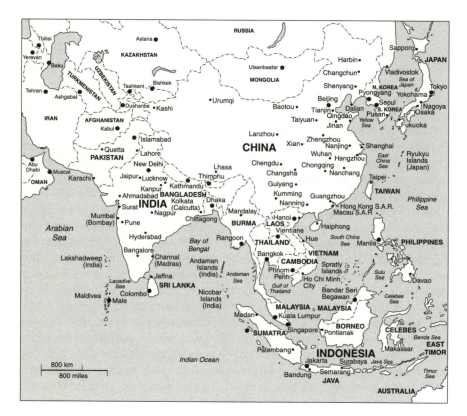

Map of Asia

Chapter 1

Introduction

What is democracy?

One of my strongest memories in high school was a required course in Washington state history and government taught by the assistant football coach, whose mastery of history was inversely proportional to his love of football. Most of us were bored silly by the class. It taught the mechanics of state government – the how – without ever bothering to explain why. We memorized the parts of the political machine of the state with about as much passionate intensity as we memorized the anatomical features of the arthropod phylum in sophomore biology across the hall. Years later, when I became a teacher myself (but not, alas, a football coach), I frequently found myself wondering how often I, too, was guilty of boring my students to death by teaching them the content of a particular subject without ever bothering to explain to them why it is important.

Fortunately for the reader, the subject of this book – democracy – lends itself readily to the most fundamental preoccupations of our daily life through its connection with the human aspiration for freedom. On this topic most people – young and old – have strong feelings. Take teenagers, for example. As they grow into adulthood they come into increasing conflict with various forms of authority that restrict the free exercise of their will. Parents, teachers, police officers all seem united in a conspiracy to suppress young people's claim to full sovereignty. For teenagers, of course, freedom means an absence of constraint: the more freedom (and less constraint) the better.

This book is going to suggest that there is another way of looking at freedom, though this perspective usually commends itself to those a bit farther along in life than teenagers, namely people who have already started to accept responsibility of one kind or another. At that point an alternative perspective begins to take shape which holds that freedom is a consequence of constraint rather than an absence of constraint. As time passes, one becomes increasingly aware that for someone to enjoy freedom, someone else has to protect it. At some point, the protector and the enjoyer merge into the same person. In this case, the constraint comes from within rather than from without. One of the great political theorists of all time, Edmund Burke, put it this way:

men are qualified for civil liberty in exact proportion to their disposition to put moral chains upon their own appetites. . . . Society cannot exist unless a controlling power upon will and appetite be placed somewhere, and the less of it there is within, the more there must be without. It is ordained in the eternal constitution of things, that men of intemperate minds cannot be free. Their passions forge their fetters.[1]

Freedom and authority

The term 'democracy' derives from a combination of the Greek words *demos*, or people, and *kratos*, or rule, to form *demokratia*, or rule by the people. It is typically contrasted with monarchy (rule by one) and oligarchy (rule by the few). Not everyone agrees on how 'many' one needs to qualify for democracy, or even on exactly what 'rule' means. Perhaps there never will be agreement on those definitions. Every example we have is affected by the contingencies of time and place and culture, and by the many flaws of human character manifested by all participants in the democratic experiment.

In arriving at a useable definition of the term for the purposes of this book, we have to be careful to avoid two extremes: the first too rigid, the second too flexible. Normally, we academics prefer precision to fuzziness. Our inclination, therefore, is to settle on a tidy definition of democracy that removes or at least reduces ambiguity. The problem with that approach arises at the margins of the definition. Out of, say, ten qualities associated with 'democracy,' how many does a given country have to have to be called a 'democracy'? Ten? Nine? Eight? What about seven and a half?

At the other end of the spectrum, we have to be careful not to come up with a definition of democracy that is so vague and all-encompassing that any government this side of a brutal dictatorship could be called a democracy. To keep things as simple as possible at this stage of our investigation, let me list a few of the characteristics of democracy generally put forward by scholars on the subject:

- Elections to office are open to participation by all citizens
- Each vote is of equal value
- Voters have real and free choices
- Citizens have open access to information
- There is a rule of law guaranteeing freedom

This list is not exhaustive, nor is it without controversy. Take the first item on the list, for example. If we take universal adult suffrage as a pre-condition for democracy, then the United States was not a democracy until the twentieth century because women were not granted the right to vote until the 19th Amendment to the US constitution was ratified in 1920, and African-Americans were not widely enfranchised until after the Civil Rights

Act of 1964. In Great Britain, as late as 1832, only 5 percent of the population was permitted to vote. And yet most historians, rightly or wrongly, and most members of the general public, would consider the US and Britain democracies in the nineteenth century. We have to be careful, therefore, in applying our criteria too narrowly.

Above all, we need to keep in mind that, in spite of its many different forms and undeniable flaws, democracy is a manifestation of one of the most fundamental aspirations of the human species for freedom. Its opposite condition – slavery – is everywhere on earth considered to be the lowest form of life. This study will proceed on the assumption that the term 'democracy' remains meaningful even though its manifestations in various cultures and times may differ from each other in significant respects. In making this claim I am reminded of a statement made by our physician when one of our children came down with a serious illness that had not been correctly diagnosed (by another doctor, actually). The doctor told us that the symptoms of any given ailment may differ in significant respects from one patient to another, and even from the textbook definition of the disease. For that reason, he pointed out, diagnosis is an art as well as a science, requiring an understanding of context as well as judgment about the relative value of the parts to the whole.

The same may truthfully be said about the enterprise of diagnosing democracy. Textbook definitions in the past have sometimes taken the position that since the institution of democracy originated in Western Europe it must therefore replicate all the characteristics of the European experience in order to be considered a valid representative of the genre. I would like to suggest a slightly different point of departure, which begins with the proposition, as I have indicated above, that freedom is one of the most fundamental attributes of the human species. The desire to be free may manifest itself in a whole range of widely differing ideas and institutions – spiritual, moral, social, economic, artistic, and political. Because this book is about democracy, we will naturally be most concerned with the political expression of the human impulse to freedom.

The second proposition is that freedom and authority are related to each other in a complementary and not adversarial way, much as the individual and the community are likewise related to each other. Neither can exist without the other, and neither can realize its full potential without the other. Freedom is the realm of the individual; authority is the realm of community. Since a good deal of the organization and evidence of this proposition, it needs to be fully understood. The conventional understanding in the West today automatically pits freedom against authority. That understanding has emerged from a common body of interpretation that harkens back to the mechanistic view of the universe that is one of the hallmarks of the scientific revolution. This mechanistic view is itself grounded in an atomistic belief that the basic building block of nature is a fully autonomous and individual unit of organization. To understand the known world is simply a case of understanding how these autonomous units are assembled. The individual unit is primary and natural, the assembled machine secondary and contrived. This mechanistic view displaced a view of the world that is often termed 'organic,' with roots in both the Judeo-Christian and the Greek traditions. According to this view, the universe is not analogous to a machine but to a living thing, which exists in dynamic interaction with its environment and which cannot be fully understood by reference only to its constituent parts. The whole is therefore more than merely the sum of its individual parts. The contemporary environmental and ecological movements in Europe and the United States are, not surprisingly, reviving this biological metaphor through their insistence on looking at the whole.

In much of the Asian tradition, the organic or ecological metaphor was never lost but remains to this day essential to the Asian way of looking at the world. In this perspective, the claims of community (of which the institution of the family is an integral part) are not secondary to those of the individual. Indeed, it is often the other way around. In some cases the community trumps the individual. My intention is not to assign praise or blame to one or the other of these views. On the contrary, my own view is that they are both valuable, and can best be seen as complementary to each other rather than mutually exclusive.

Another way of getting at this perspective is through an African proverb which says that where something stands, something else always stands beside it. Nothing, in other words, can be fully understood without some comparative context. By the same token, where freedom stands, authority always stands beside it. The more freedom one has, the more authority is necessary to protect it; conversely, the more authority one has, the more freedom is necessary to balance the equation. Thus it is, as I explain more fully below, that without the authority of custom, law, and morality, freedom would cease to exist altogether; and without freedom of choice, the authority of custom, law, and morality would no longer be possible. Exactly how that dynamic plays itself out in the growth of Asian democracy is the subject of this book.

This view – that the relationship between freedom and authority was primarily complementary and not adversarial – was also part of the Western tradition in its formative stages. Plato and Aristotle, it turns out, had many of the same reservations about bestowing freedom on the masses as our parents did about bestowing freedom on us, and as we do on our own children. In all cases there was some question as to whether the average subject's judgment is sufficiently developed to take on responsibility for self-governance. Indeed, why freedom in the first place? When we are very young (say, until the age of two!), we accept the authority of our parents without question. They are, after all, the 'author' of us in the most basic physical sense imaginable. In time, however, children develop greater confidence in their own faculties of judgment. At some point they begin to challenge the authority of their parents and assert their own will. That point may differ from culture to culture, and in some cultures the younger generation may choose to obey the older generation for a very long time, but in America the process begins in teenagehood.

Many teenagers, in the midst of their struggles with authority, begin to look upon authority as the natural enemy of freedom. That conclusion is perfectly understandable, since it is some representative of authority that is standing in the way of their freedom of choice. Freedom, in that context, readily becomes defined, as I have suggested above, as an absence of constraint. In so doing teenagers are actually adopting a position that emerged in the West during the Renaissance when intellectuals abandoned a preoccupation with religious issues for more secular concerns. Whereas political philosophers during the Middle Ages had been focused on the moral and religious dimensions of politics, Renaissance thinkers like Niccolò Machiavelli changed the terms of discourse to confine politics exclusively to the realm of power. If the art of politics is about nothing more than how to get or retain power, then it is a short journey to the conclusion that the world is divided into those who have power and those who don't. Those who have power dictate constraints to those who don't have power. The adversarial relationship is inescapable.

This book will take a different tack and assert that freedom and authority are partners, not enemies. I will argue that each depends on the other, even for its very existence. In political terms, the authority of the state makes the freedom of the citizen possible and the freedom of the citizen makes the authority of the state possible. Without one there cannot be the other. The relative degree of each may vary from time to time and place to place. An excess of freedom and a deficiency of authority produces anarchy. An excess of authority and a deficiency of freedom produces tyranny. A balance produces good government. How that balance is achieved and preserved, particularly in modern Asia, is the subject of this book. By looking at the Asian experience we will gain a better understanding of how democratic institutions might be fostered in those parts of the world in which they do not presently exist, and how they might be strengthened in those parts of the world (such as the United States) where they exist but are often taken so much for granted they may thereby be endangered.

This study rests upon a simple thesis: namely that through understanding the mutually dependent relationship of freedom and authority one can acquire a new and fresh perspective on the evolution of democratic institutions around the world. The aspiration for freedom is one of the most precious and defining characteristics of the human species. It manifests itself in every realm of human endeavor – social, economic, religious, techno-logical, and political. Without freedom, all the tools and arts of civilization that surround us would never have come into being. We are in every way the children of freedom.

Moving from the universal to the particular, this study has a major sub-theme in the form of an assertion that historical experience and cultural values, in addition to political and economic conditions, have played a leading role in preparing the way for democracy in Asia by framing the larger context of moral authority within which freedom can flourish. Writers on the subject of democracy generally tend to be journalists or academic specialists in government or political science. Understandably they focus on political institutions. By itself this is not mistaken, but that approach overlooks a broader array of factors whose influence may not be direct but whose cumulative effect is nevertheless significant. Until now many characteristics of Asian cultures – especially the emphasis on authority – have been assumed by Western scholars to favor despotism. Both Karl Marx and his modern protagonist Karl Wittfogel believed that Asian political institutions were incurably autocratic. According to their interpretation, the centralized form of government that appeared in the early stages of Asian civilizations had suppressed the development of pluralistic institutions and produced a centralized form of government known as 'oriental despotism.'[2] After the state gained a monopoly of power, rulers had no incentive to surrender control and the people no opportunity to seize it.

There is much to be said for this, but it does not paint a complete picture, as Edward Said discusses at length and with brilliant insight in his masterpiece *Orientalism*.[3] For one thing, in spite of the emphasis on the rule of law in the West, autocratic rule was also the norm throughout its existence until the very recent past. For another, in Asia where the rule of law was less valued, morality provided a strong counterpoint. In Chinese society, for example, although civil law played no role in enforcing acceptable behavior, social sanctions were imposed by the community according to a Confucian ethical code, as well as local customs. The Confucians believed that laws would only challenge people to evade them, while moral principles would make laws unnecessary. The former was imposed from the outside, the latter from the inside. This view was once also common in the Western tradition – Thucydides in fifth-century Athens believed that the downfall of Athenian democracy was caused primarily by a breakdown in the moral fiber of Athenian society (for which the primary catalyst was the plague). In any case, most Confucian political philosophers have believed that public morality was the indispensable basis of all good government.

To be sure, the issue of the connection between public morality and democracy was never far from the Western mind as well, and I don't mean to over-state my case. Thinkers such as Alexis de Tocqueville and statesmen such as Woodrow Wilson have had similar preoccupations in modern times. Tocqueville was concerned that the American commitment to radical individualism would eventually undermine the social ties on which civic responsibility depended. President Wilson was reluctant to permit the United States to join the Great War because he feared a prolonged conflict would undermine the standards of public morality that formed the indispensable foundation of democracy. The American philosopher John Dewey believed that a moral education was equally indispensable for the health and survival of our democratic form of government, and dedicated his scholarly life to promoting the connections between education and democracy. Nevertheless, in the main Western societies have tended to argue that any assertion of moral value compromises the freedom of the individual conscience.[4]

The relevance of this issue to the subject of Asian democracy lies in the new insights it reveals into the nature of democracy itself. If it varies so much in practice from age to age and from culture to culture, what remains common to all? What are the essentials and accidentals of democracy? What are the enabling ideas and institutions without which it cannot flourish? What are the threats to its survival? Are these threats primarily internal? Are the champions of democracy justified in their assertion of its universal applicability? Does nationalism – arguably the greatest threat to peace in the coming century – threaten to undermine the foundations of a just democracy? When all is said and done, what can we learn from the experience of other cultures?

Equality

Democracy is based, to some degree, on the principle of human equality. It presupposes that all citizens, regardless of social status or economic wealth or political power, stand as equals at the ballot box. This view does not deny the existence of natural differences between individuals. Clearly some are smarter than others. Some have more relevant experience on specific issues than others. Others have, through their wealth, unusual leverage over the instruments of persuasion and control. But on election day, these differences are, to an important degree, set aside. If all citizens are equal in one sense and unequal in others, what does the term really mean?

Political philosophers are in the habit of dividing equality into two kinds: equality of condition and equality of opportunity. The former meaning, as its name implies, rests on the assumption that people ought to live in a manner that minimizes their differences. Taken to an extreme this interpretation would imply that everyone should live in houses and wear clothes that cost a similar amount, have roughly the same incomes, indulge in similar leisure activities, and so forth. In general, the socialist movement of the last two centuries, beginning with Jean-Jacques Rousseau in the late eighteenth century, has tended to emphasize this aspect of equality. At one end of the spectrum were socialists who believed (and some still do) that the source of human inequality was private property. The abolition of private property, which Karl Marx advocated in the nineteenth century, would therefore usher in a new age of human equality. But not all socialists advocated such extreme measures. The graduated income tax that Americans have long come to accept as a natural part of the landscape was adopted from the socialist platform, and represents one mechanism to foster equality of condition in the United States. It was one of many policies, such as unemployment benefits, adopted by the United States that originated in the European socialist movement.

The other definition of equality stresses opportunity. It rests on the assumption that all human beings are endowed with a fundamental dignity that derives from the qualities present in each person in potential form at the beginning of life. It is therefore the responsibility of the community into which each person is born to provide institutions that nurture the human potential of its members. At some point, when the child becomes an adult, he or she begins to share in the responsibility for developing that potential in the upcoming generation. Fundamental to the democratic principle is an understanding of the special worth of each person and the right of all persons to develop and express their potential in an atmosphere of respect for equality of opportunity. Although the two kinds of equality are different in theory, in practice they often are smooshed together. Inequality of condition caused by poverty, for example, will often raise such barriers to minimal standards of health and education that the prospect of equality of opportunity becomes a cruel joke. Both forms of equality, incidentally, share the same root meaning as equity (i.e., fairness or justice).

In the West the understanding of human equality, and its subsidiary doctrine of human rights, derives from two sources: the Judeo-Christian tradition and the Greek philosophy of Stoicism. The early Hebrew belief that human beings were created in the image of God – enshrined in the book of Genesis – conferred upon each human individual a special dignity. All humankind was understood to share a common origin and a common nature. What God conferred no human agency could remove. The belief that we are all children of God, and therefore deserve to be treated with respect, has exerted an enormous influence on the evolution of institutions in Western civilization, no matter how often it may have been violated in practice. The fact that such an ideal may be honored more in the breach than the observance, or that it may be widely and consistently abused, does not mean that it has no relevance in an imperfect world. The present doctrine of human rights in the West, which has done so much to elevate the expectations we apply to rulers in our own time, would be unthinkable without the religious heritage of Judaism and Christianity.

The later Christian views on equality and politics, in turn, were themselves influenced by the Greek doctrine of Stoicism. Stoicism arose in Hellenistic Greece after the classical age of fifth-century BC Athens and after the death of Aristotle (in 322 BC). It originated around 300 BC with Zeno of Citium, at least one of whose parents was not Greek but Phoenician. According to one historian, Stoicism centered around the fundamental ideas of the unity of the human race, the equality of man and therefore justice in the state, the equal worth of men and women, respect for the rights of wives and children, benevolence, love, purity in the family, tolerance and charity toward our fellows, humanity in all cases.[5]

This view represented a significant departure from Aristotle's assertion that women, foreigners, and slaves, should be excluded from participation in the public life of the community by virtue of their inferior status, and that only male citizens possessed a legitimate claim to equality.

The second major proponent of Stoicism was Chryssipus (*c.* 280–207 BC). He was followed by Panaetius who introduced the philosophy to Rome where it was set to beautiful Latin prose by the Roman statesman Cicero. Chryssipus argued that no man is a slave by nature, that slavery violates a fundamental natural law which is universal in scope. This notion of a law of nature transcending the positive law of a particular state became a powerful tool of reform and criticism in Western civilization. Indeed, the contrast between a universal standard of justice common to all and the positive civil law of a particular state is nowhere more apparent than in the subject of slavery, and suggests an opportunity for hypocrisy. Cicero kept slaves. For that matter, so did Thomas Jefferson, whose following remark certainly suggests that he understood the distinction between natural law (or justice) and positive law, even if he chose not to follow the former in his personal life:

> I tremble for my country when I reflect that God is just, that his justice cannot sleep forever. Commerce between master and slave is despotism. Nothing is more certainly written in the book of fate than that these people are to be free.[6]

All the same, it would be a mistake to conclude that because people like Jefferson didn't live up to their ideals, the ideals were therefore meaningless. Over time, they exerted a powerful if often indirect influence on the conduct of everyday affairs, and still do.

Stoicism came into being in a world in which the autonomous city-state had ceased to exist and had been recently replaced by the new form of universal empire created by Alexander the Great (who died in 323 BC). The new political order brought together peoples from different cultures on a scale so manifestly greater than that of the city-state, and so different from one other in language, custom, and history, that the previous categories of politics were no longer adequate to achieve a basis for a political commonwealth. Stoicism, with its inclusive and universal outlook, was the intellectual expression of the same universalizing energy in politics that produced the new institution of empire. The Stoics believed that human beings are born into two communities, the nation of their birth (e.g., the *polis*) and the universal community of all humankind (i.e., the *cosmopolis*). All humankind is therefore a composite of qualities that are unique (such as individual attributes of tallness or shortness as well as cultural attributes of language and custom) and qualities that are shared with all other human beings (such as a rational and social nature). It is the latter quality that makes possible human society on a larger scale than that of the city-state. It is also universal characteristics of all humans embodied in Stoic philosophy that justified the claim of equality which we now associate with the democratic ethic. This perception that all people are endowed by nature with certain potentials, and therefore deserve to be treated with a basic level of dignity proportional to the preciousness of the gift which nature has bestowed upon them, became one of the cornerstones of Western democracy.

Although the institution of democracy originated in the West, with its understandings of equality informed by both religious tradition and philosophical heritage, it would be a mistake to infer that the Asian tradition does not also have its own equivalent perspective. One of the central characteristics of all the major world religions is a profound sense of the dignity of the individual human person. Each human being is endowed with a special gift to apprehend the divine, together with the freedom to develop that gift or to reject it. Even Hinduism, which to the Western observer seems so hierarchical in its ascending levels of worthiness embodied in the caste system, shares that underlying bedrock belief in the hope that any person can eventually reach spiritual perfection. Buddhism was itself founded in part as an assertion of equality. Islam, as well, reflects a profound sense in the underlying equality of all human beings. In terms of theory, Muhammad was reputed to have said that people are as 'equal as the teeth of a comb.'[7] In terms of practice, the heritage of appealing to *shurah* (consultation), *ijma* (consensus), and *ijtihad* (independent interpretive judgment) in determining the standards of behavior to which the members of the community are enjoined to conform, could readily be use to support the development of Islamic institutions of democracy.[8] The great religious traditions of the world, therefore, are rich and diverse entities, with plenty of room for a democratic theory to be derived from them.

What are the institutional ingredients of democracy?

Institutions, taken as a whole, constitute the womb of political freedom. Just as the rules of grammar and the habits of vocabulary make possible the expressive freedom of language, so do rules and laws and habits of compromise in politics make democracy possible. The laws that limit our freedom are the very laws that also protect our freedom. Indeed, without those laws, or habits, democracy would cease to exist. But only certain kinds of laws make possible certain kinds of freedom. What laws, or rules, which come to be embodied in 'institutions' (such as legal institutions, political institutions, etc.), give rise to democracy?

The Yale scholar Robert A. Dahl, one of the preeminent specialists on democracy, has identified six major institutional prerequisites for what he calls 'full democracy':[9]

- Elected officials
- Free, fair, and frequent elections
- Freedom of expression
- Alternative sources of information
- Associational autonomy
- Inclusive citizenship

The first category defines representative democracy, which differs from its ancestor in classical Greece – direct democracy – in that the business of government is conducted by representatives of the electorate, not by the citizens themselves. The second category concerns the process of elections. One can easily imagine a situation, for which history provides multiple examples, in which a ruler might conduct elections with only one viable candidate for each office. He would therefore be satisfying the first prerequisite but not the second. The third category means exactly what it says, that citizens have the right to criticize those in power without fear of retribution. The fourth category acknowledges the potential for a given government to undermine the substance of democracy by monopolizing control over the information available to the citizenry. The fifth category reflects the importance of citizens being allowed to associate with each other in groups and parties that are not con-trolled by the government. The final category recognizes that access to the rights and responsibilities of governance needs to be universally available to all inhabitants of a state, limited only by the experience of common sense (children, for example, being probably best excluded from participation until they reach a certain age of maturity and judgment).

What are the conditions for democracy?

The various prerequisites listed above may appear in different proportions at different times in different countries. Not all of them were possessed by governments we still refer to as democracies, such as that of ancient Athens (or even in the US in the nineteenth century, where women were not allowed to vote). Taken together, they form a template that we can then apply to specific cases considered in this book, allowing us to categorize governments as 'partially' or 'fully' democratic with some reasonable measure of precision. It is worth pointing out that the full complement of all six criteria, namely representative democracy with universal suffrage, did not exist before in human history until the twentieth century.

This fact is important to remember as we consider the rise of democratic institutions in Asia. Many Western observers, in their eagerness to claim the invention of democracy, forget that its early appearance in the 'West' was not only temporary but also categorically different from its modern form. Accustomed as we are now to regard the rough and tumble of party politics as a natural and perhaps desirable manifestation of the democratic process at work, such conflict was once regarded as harmful factionalism. Such a view was apparent even in Athens, the home of Western democracy. Plato and Aristotle believed that factionalism would undermine the body politic. Certainly it was so believed in the early years of the American republic, when George Washington condemned the very factionalism that later led to the rise of political parties in the United States. The same was also true in China, where well-known political factions, such as the Donglin movement in the late Ming dynasty (during the sixteenth and seventeenth centuries), and the Self-Strengthening Movement in the late Qing dynasty (during the nineteenth century), were often interpreted in negative terms as disturbing the harmony of the body politic. Today we might see them differently, as representing a positive force for enhancing public participation in politics, though without the name and legitimacy of a 'party' in the modern sense.

So, having reviewed many different paths that some countries have followed to arrive at the same destination of democracy, we should not be surprised to discover considerable diversity in terms of the overall conditions favorable to the development of democracy. What are those conditions? They can be usefully divided into two general categories: essential and favorable.[10] Essential conditions include the following:

- Civilian control of the military and police
- Democratic political culture
- Absence of intervention by foreign powers

Insuring that the armed forces and the police are under the control of elected officials is one of the most important and necessary conditions for democracy. The beginning of the end of the Roman republic occurred when the general Lucius Cornelius Sulla used military force to take power in Rome in 88 BC. Even though he subsequently implemented reforms designed to strengthen the power of the Senate, his precedent in usurping power was followed by so many later leaders that the republic was already a corpse by the time Augustus took over the state in 27 BC. This phenomenon of the military taking over a government in order to punish corrupt politicians or restore 'order' – thereby undermining the foundations of democracy – is a frequent phenomenon in the history of Asian as well as Western democracies, as we will see in later chapters of this book.

The second category of essential conditions for democracy – democratic political culture – refers simply to the sum total of the habits of thought and action in a civil society that embody democratic principles. One of the compelling arguments for the remarkable success of democracy in India, for example, is the existence of a long tradition in rural India of peasants electing leaders who preside over the affairs of each village in institutions such as the *panchayat* and the *sabha*. Conversely, one of the reasons given for the weakness of democracy in Weimar Germany after the First World War is the absence of a political culture that favored democratic ways of thinking.

The third category is absence of intervention by foreign powers. During the Cold War between 1945–1990, both the United States and the Soviet Union intervened to suppress democratic movements in states that fell under their sphere of influence. Eastern Europe was dominated by the Soviet Union, while in Latin America and Africa the United States supported and in some cases installed in office a number of dictators simply because they were anti-communist. Although both superpowers claimed to be in favor of democracy (though with very different definitions of the term!), in practice they placed a higher priority on their own national interest. To be sure, living under the totalitarian rule of the USSR (wherein all aspects of life were controlled by the state) was far more destructive of human freedom than living under a dictator propped up by the US (wherein only political aspects of life were controlled by the state). In any case, my main point here is that the Cold War imposed an atmosphere of fear on global politics that often caused democratic states to act in very undemocratic ways.

The above essential conditions are those without which democracy cannot survive. In addition, there are a number of conditions that are conducive to democracy but are, by themselves, not essential. These favorable conditions for the development of democracy include:

• Market economy
• Cultural homogeneity
• Rule of law
• Peace

The contributions of a capitalist market economy to the success of democracy are many. The most important are two: economic prosperity and the rise of a middle class. Economic prosperity provides the basic foundation of stability that facilitates cooperation between the members of a given society. When most people have jobs, when there is a level of general prosperity sufficient to pay for public services of high quality such as schools, when people are reasonably satisfied with their material surroundings, then the general public is more disposed to take part in public affairs than if these conditions are absent. Confidence in the future inspires respect for others, which is the foundation for compromise on which all democratic institutions rest. As the fruits of prosperity multiply in market economies, those who fall into the category of the middle class grow in number and confidence. They are the soldiers of democracy. They are the ones who vote and who participate in associations of all kinds that taken together form the political culture of democracy.

A market economy, however, is not an unmixed blessing. To be sure, the prosperity it brings is an indisputable contribution to the success of democracy. We shall see that dynamic at work over and over again in Asia in the twentieth century. But that prosperity is not always distributed equitably. On the contrary, by stressing competition over cooperation and by basing its institutional structure on the free exercise of choice, a market economy often undermines the commitment to equality that democracies depend upon for their long-term stability. When the gap between the rich and the poor in capitalist societies reaches a point where those on the bottom feel disenfranchised, the stability of the system as a whole will be threatened. Brazilian democracy, with its massive disparities in income between the richest and the poorest, lives in perpetual danger of collapse. Socialist economies, on the other hand, face a reverse problem – their commitment to equality tends to undermine the freedoms and incentives that promote economic productivity. In Cuba, for example, everyone may be equal, but they are equally poor.

In the United States, a two-party system has balanced this natural tension between freedom and equality in an interesting way. As a rule, the Republican party has tended to define justice in terms of freedom, while the Democratic party has tended to define justice in terms of equality. The benefit of this arrangement is that over time they rotate in office so that the two scales of Lady Justice – freedom and equality – remain roughly in balance. The drawback is that the rhetoric of the two parties, both of which focus on justice but define it in different terms, often seems to generate more heat than light as representatives of the two parties talk past each other, using the same words but investing them with different meanings.

The issue of cultural homogeneity is complex. There are certainly examples of successful democracies – such as Switzerland and even Canada – composed of different linguistic or ethnic groups. For the most part, however, those examples are the exception. In most cases democracy flourishes more successfully in a country with some degree of cultural homogeneity. To understand why this is so requires more space than we have here. Suffice to say that the desire to be part of a community is one of the most essential characteristics of the human species. The community is the stage on which the human potential is enabled to fulfill itself. Part of being in a community, however, is becoming aware of differences with other communities. The habits of trust and compromise on which democracy is based are easier to foster within a homogeneous community than a heterogeneous one. This criterion is not meant to exclude the possibility of multicultural democracy, but rather to suggest those qualities that contribute to a successful outcome. Given that there are already so many grounds for conflict and misunderstanding between citizens and groups of citizens in a given polity, together with the undeniable tendency of people to distinguish between 'us' and 'them,' a pronounced cultural heterogeneity is a positive obstacle to achieving the degree of social unity that democracy requires for its survival.

The United States is a case in point. On the one hand, it is an amazingly diverse society, a veritable sea into which all the rivers of the world's peoples have flowed. The descendants of Europeans are now rapidly approaching minority status, and there are cleavages in American society along racial and economic lines that threaten to break the ties that bind the country together. On the other hand, its fundamental institutions and its language – essential ingredients to foster a sense of shared community – remain those of its European forebears. In addition, Americans remain united by an idea of human freedom that permeates all aspects of daily life and to which its most revered leaders from Thomas Jefferson to Abraham Lincoln to Martin Luther King have paid tribute. The perpetual and ceaseless challenge is to find the right balance. In the end, too much homogeneity stifles freedom; too little undermines unity.

A rule of law is a necessary condition for democracy simply because without it there is no guarantee of fairness in the application of rules. Without a minimal expectation of fairness, compromise and cooperation become too risky for the common citizen to practice. Without compromise and cooperation, democracy cannot thrive. The widespread corruption that plagues public life in Russia and the republics of the former Soviet Union represent a significant threat to the long-term viability of democracy in those regions. Similarly, the absence of a rule of law in China is a major obstacle to the development of democracy.

Peace, which all of those who have never lived through war have a tendency to take for granted, is yet another condition for the health and survival of democracy. The moral and economic collapse that followed the end of the First World War in Europe did indeed weaken the foundations of democracy across the continent to such a degree that Adolf Hitler rode to power almost effortlessly. His victory then led to yet another war of even greater ferocity. Simply put, war demeans all who are involved – the victor and the vanquished. The greater the destruction, the greater the overall diminishment of the human spirit. Some would argue that Western civilization was wounded mortally by the ferocity and horror of war in the twentieth century. The historian Jacques Barzun, for example, looking out over the perspective of the last 500 years of European history, offers the thesis that the First World War precipitated a period of decadence in Western civilization from which it has not yet fully recovered.[11] The widespread materialism, the propensity for violence in the media, the consumerism of popular culture, are merely the visible consequences of a process of spiritual decline. One can only hope that the decades of relative peace since those cataclysmic spasms of violence have healed some of those wounds. One can also imagine that Europeans, having themselves tasted the bitterness of war on their own land, are far more aware of the dangers to democracy than Americans, who have had the luxury of always fighting their wars on someone else's land, and who now possess such a preponderance of global power that they are in grave danger of succumbing to the very same temptations of pride and arrogance that brought Athens to ruin in the Peloponnesian War.

Conclusion

By understanding the institutional prerequisites and the enabling conditions of democracy that have been covered in this chapter, we can better appreciate the variety of democracy around the globe and through time. To speak of democracy it is best to think in terms of a continuum that ranges from full-scale tyranny on the one end, through partial or hybrid democracies of various kinds, to full democracies on the other end of the spectrum. Different scholars may choose different points along the spectrum to mark the threshold of democracy. In a sense, no one has reached the end of the spectrum. No one can claim to have arrived if for no other reason than that democracy is not a destination but a process which requires constant renewal. Where one locates any given country on this continuum is probably not as important as it is to have a clear sense of the complexity of the issues involved.

One of the main objectives of this book is for the reader to come away with a deeper appreciation for the variety of democratic institutions throughout the world. The underlying principle is that we can all learn from each other. Just as Asia can benefit from the European respect for law and the individual as a basis for democratic rights, so can Europeans and Americans benefit from the Asian respect for ethics and community as a basis for democratic responsibility. It is difficult to imagine democracy in East Asia succeeding without the cultural heritage of Confucianism; it is equally difficult to imagine democracy in South Asia succeeding without the leadership of people like Mahatma Gandhi and Jawaharlal Nehru, whose moral authority was itself grounded in the ethical and spiritual values of the Indian tradition. To be sure, all of these nations, including our own, have sometimes fallen so short of their ideals as to call into question whether the ideals have any motivating power whatsoever. I believe they do.

The second objective of this book is for the reader to develop a heightened awareness of the human need for freedom and of the value of moral and political authority that enable human freedom to exist and flourish. The great French intellectual Raymond Aron once remarked that 'freedom is the strongest and most enduring desire of all mankind.'[12] Freedom itself may be defined in starkly different terms even by members of the same culture. Some will interpret freedom as an absence of restraint. Others will interpret it as a complete surrender to the will of God. But the desire to be free is universal. Through understanding democracy we can cultivate a deeper awareness of our shared humanity and our common destiny.

Notes

1 'Letter to a Member of the French National Assembly,' *The Works of the Right Honourable Edmund Burke*, vol. 6 (London, 1826), p. 64.
2 The relevant work is Karl Wittfogel, *Oriental Despotism* (New Haven: Yale University Press, 1959).
3 Edward Said, *Orientalism* (New York: Vintage, 1979).
4 A fascinating treatment of this very issue can be found in Peter Berkowitz, *Virtue and the Making of Modern Liberalism* (Princeton: Princeton University Press, 1999).
5 Jacques Denis, quoted in George Sabine, *A History of Political Theory* (Hinsdale, IL: Dryden Press, 1973), p. 152.
6 These words are engraved on the side of the Jefferson Monument in Washington, DC, and are quoted from Kenneth Clark, *Civilisation* (New York: Harper and Row, 1969), p. 268.
7 Quoted in Fethullah Gülen, 'A Comparative Approach to Islam and Democracy,' *SAIS Review* (2001), p. 134.
8 See the excellent study by John L. Esposito and John O. Voll, *Islam and Democracy* (New York: Oxford University Press, 1996), p. 27.
9 *On Democracy* (New Haven: Yale University Press, 1998), pp. 85–86.
10 See Robert A. Dahl, *On Democracy* (New Haven: Yale University Press, 1998), pp. 145–165.
11 *From Dawn to Decadence* (New York: HarperCollins, 2000). Note especially the following comment: 'It was not long after the end of the Great War that farseeing observers predicted the likelihood of another and it became plain that western civilization had brought itself into a condition from which full recovery was unlikely. The devastation, both material and moral, had gone so deep that it turned the creative energies from their course, first into frivolity, and then into the channel of self-destruction' (p. 712).
12 *Democracy and Totalitarianism* (New York, 1965), p. 229. Quoted in Donald Treadgold, *Freedom: A History* (New York: New York University Press, 1990), p. 416.

Further reading

An accessible introduction to democracy for the general reader, by one of the giants in the field, is *On Democracy* by Robert A. Dahl (New Haven: Yale University Press, 1998). A more detailed approach, by the same author, is *Democracy and its Critics* (New Haven: Yale University Press, 1989). See also Benjamin R. Barber, *Strong Democracy: Participatory Politics for a New Age* (Berkeley: University of California Press, 1984), and Amy Gutmann, *Liberal Equality* (Cambridge: Cambridge University Press, 1980). For a classic statement on human equality, there are two great texts: Jean-Jacques Rousseau's *Social Contract*, and his *Essay on the Origins of Inequality*. One of the great essays on democracy is John Stuart Mill's *Considerations on Representative Government*. A helpful collection of Tocqueville's writings on the subject are contained in *Alexis de Tocqueville: On Democracy, Revolution, and Society*, edited by John Stone and Stephen Mennell (Chicago: University of Chicago Press, 1980). For a passionate defense of equality and its relationship to democracy see Philip Green's *Equality and Democracy* (New York: The New Press, 1998). Every year Freedom House publishes an excellent country-by-country assessment of freedom around the world entitled *Freedom in the World: Annual Survey of Political Rights and Civil*

Liberties. An invaluable reference is *Democracy in Asia and Africa*, edited by Seymour Martin Lipset (Washington, DC: Congressional Quarterly, 1998). The quarterly academic journal *Journal of Democracy*, published by Johns Hopkins University Press, is extremely helpful. Two useful surveys of democracy are Roland N. Stromberg's *Democracy: A Short, Analytical History* (Armonk: M.E. Sharpe, 1996); and Sanford Lakoff's *Democracy: History, Theory, Practice* (Boulder: Westview Press, 1996). There is a growing and, of course, constantly changing array of websites on the Internet devoted to democracy. A good beginning can be found with the following sites:

www.ceip.org Democracy and Rule of Law Project at the Carnegie Endowment for International Peace.
www.ned.org National Endowment for Democracy.
http://usinfo.state.gov/topical/rights Democracy and Human Rights, US Department of State.
www.democ.uci.edu/democ/ Center for the Study of Democracy at UC Irvine.
www.freedomhouse.org/ Freedom House.
www.amnesty.org/ailib/index.html Amnesty International country reports.
www.hrw.org/wr2k/ Human Rights Watch world reports.
www.nipissingu.ca/department/history/muhlberger/histdem/index.htm Professor Steven Muhlberger's website at Nipissing University on the world history of democracy.

Chapter 2

The rise of democracy in Europe

Modern democracy, as it came into existence in Western Europe and then spread to North America, derived from four principal antecedents: hunting/gathering societies, classical Greece, republican Rome, and Renaissance Italy. The last three were narrowly confined in terms of both space and time. In most of recorded history the concept of democracy – as we now understand it today – was either unknown or considered an inferior form of government. Nevertheless, those few cases where democracy was given a chance shared a fundamental commitment to the value of public participation in decisions affecting the general welfare of the community. Only in the nineteenth century was it transferred to the nation-state, where it began to assume its present shape.

Hunting-gathering societies

The origin of humankind remains clouded in mystery and is a subject of much controversy among anthropologists. Simply put, the first hominids appeared over 4 million years ago. About 2.5 million years ago, the first members of the genus *Homo* evolved, known as *Homo habilis*, followed by its larger-brained descendent *Homo erectus* about 1.8 million years ago. The first members of the species *Homo sapiens* arrived approximately 400,000 years ago, followed by modern humans, *Homo sapiens sapiens*, approximately 100,000 years ago (and quite probably before). The archeological evidence currently suggests that *Homo habilis* was most likely a scavenger, and that hunting, together with the domestication of fire, did not become common until the arrival of *Homo erectus*.

The simple fact that for almost two million years the human species lived as hunter-gatherers has given rise to a relatively new branch of academic research known as evolutionary psychology. Proponents of this theory hold that the basic characteristics of humankind were formed during this long period, and that our current patterns of behavior are much more profoundly affected by our tradition of hunting and gathering than we realize. This is not the place to engage in a discussion of the merits of that assertion. If there are elements of truth in it, however, then we should not exclude it from our discussion of human freedom and democracy.

The central identifying characteristic of hunting-gathering societies was the sharing of food. Social structures were close and cooperative. Since the size of the social units in such societies was around 25–50 people, and since the amount of time necessary to gather sufficient food is estimated to have averaged little more than twenty hours a week, the interactions among the individuals in the group were intense. Decision-making involved extensive consultation and participation by most members of the community. Based in part on inferences made from the archeological evidence as well as from observation of contemporary hunting-gathering societies, these bands appear to have been remarkably egalitarian. It was not until after the domestication of plants, when the increased food supply made it possible for much larger communities to exist, that complex systems of hierarchy appeared.

Humans developed these systems of hierarchy in order to cope with the more complex challenges of storing food, protecting the community from attack by outsiders, providing for adequate sewerage, among many other tasks. The practice of public participation in decision-making receded into the background in proportion as the communities grew in complexity. 'Democracy,' insofar as the term had any meaning at the time apart from participation by most members of the community in decision-making, disappeared for thousands of years. Nevertheless, that long period of development must have had a profound impact on the human psyche. Evolutionary psychologists have argued just that, namely that because the human species spent 99.4 percent of its existence as hunter-gatherers in roughly egalitarian circumstances calling for intense forms of human communication and participation, we developed a natural disposition in the human personality for just those kinds of activities, making the current phase of democratization not so much a new development as a renaissance of something very hallowed in our past.

Ancient Greece

The Greeks are given credit for having provided the first example of democracy in complex sedentary societies. Although democratic institutions are generally assumed to have first appeared in the city-state of Athens in 507 BC, there is some reason to believe that the institution of a popular assembly (*ekklesia*) actually arose in the Greek city-state of Sparta a century earlier. There is some irony in that provenance, since it was also Sparta that defeated Athens in the Peloponnesian War in 404 BC. Following that defeat, Athens did experience a period of internal democracy for a few decades until it eventually fell under the suzerainty of Alexander the Great's empire. The Macedonian overlords of the Greeks were soon followed by the Romans, the Byzantines, and finally the

Ottomans. Not until the nineteenth century did the Greeks recapture their freedom, and only in the twentieth century did they once again, after an absence of more than two thousand years, regain democratic rule.

To understand the significance of the Greek achievement in democratic rule one must first understand exactly how it developed and operated. Greek politics in the sixth and fifth centuries BC was centered around the institution of the city-state, or *polis*, which constituted the basic political unit of the day as well as an urban center. Though Sparta seems to have developed institutions of public participation in government earlier than did Athens, Athens later brought them to a much higher state. The origins of democracy in Athens lie in institutions that were created by the statesman Cleisthenes (570–507 BC). Cleisthenes broke the back of the entrenched aristocracy in Athens by substituting location for kinship as the basic unit of representation. He divided the administration of the *polis* into ten tribes, each of which sent 50 representatives to a council of 500 citizens known as the *boule*. The basic principle of this body was that each citizen had an equal right to be represented.

This level of participation is remarkable when one considers that the area under the jurisdiction of Athens was approximately 1,000 sq. miles, equivalent to the state of Rhode Island, consisting of a total population of about 35–40,000 adult male citizens. We can safely assume that fewer than half, and maybe about a third of that population, lived in the cities of Athens and Piraeus, so that the rest would have had to walk some distance in order to participate in governance. But every citizen – educated or not – had the right to join in the work of the Assembly, which had the final decision on all important matters dealing with the business of government. It met outdoors and was often attended by thousands of citizens. The president of the Assembly held office for one day only, and was chosen by lot. Administrative functions were accomplished by individuals chosen also by lot, not by elections. It was difficult, under this regime, to remain a passive observer of politics and not an active participant, since personal choice played little role. Citizenship brought responsibility, from which there was no easy escape.

This participation in the Assembly reveals one of the essential characteristics of Greek democracy, namely that it was *direct*, not *representative*. Though executive functions were performed by representatives chosen by lot, the final authority rested with the Assembly. Familiarity with the principal public issues of the day was therefore shared by a very wide spectrum of the population, since at any moment they might be called to serve in one capacity or another. This system, however unwieldy it might seem to our modern sensibilities that revere specialized expertise, appears to have worked exceedingly well. According to the great classical scholar M.I. Finley, 'Athens managed for nearly two hundred years to be the most prosperous, most powerful, most stable, most peaceful internally, and culturally by far the richest state in all the Greek world.'[1]

The heroic age of Greek democracy occurred during the leadership of Pericles from approximately 462–431 BC, whose funeral oration contains one of the most stirring affirmations of human freedom and equality ever delivered:

> Let me say that our system of government does not copy the institutions of our neighbors. It is more the case of our being a model to others, than of our imitating anyone else. Our constitution is called a democracy because power is in the hands not of a minority but of the whole people. When it is a question of settling private disputes, everyone is equal before the law; when it is a question of putting one person before another in positions of public responsibility, what counts is not membership of a particular class, but the actual ability which the man possesses. No one, so long as he has it in him to be of service to the state, is kept in political obscurity because of poverty. . . . We are free and tolerant in our private lives; but in public affairs we keep to the law. This is because it commands our deep respect. . . . Here each individual is interested not only in his own affairs but in the affairs of the state as well: even those who are mostly occupied with their own business are extremely well-informed on general politics – this is a peculiarity of ours: we do not say that a man who takes no interest in politics is a man who minds his own business; we say that he has no business here at all.[2]

After Pericles came the disastrous loss to Sparta in the Peloponnesian War in 404 BC. From 403 to 322 BC there followed almost a century of stable democracy in Athens. Although Athenian power was circumscribed, there were no civil wars or deep disturbances to civic life. It was during this period that the foundations of all later Western philosophy were laid by Plato and Aristotle. After the death of Alexander the Great in 323 BC, Macedonian generals ruled Athens directly and the long run of Athenian democracy was over.

All in all, the Greeks made a number of profound contributions to the democratic tradition. They believed that humans are social animals and that their potential can be fully developed only through participating as free citizens in a political community. This point of view, in turn, rested on an optimistic faith in the human capacity for reasoned judgment, provided that it was cultivated by a rigorous education designed to foster civic virtue. This point is difficult to overemphasize. It is indeed remarkable, even in our own age, to imagine a system that places so much confidence in the judgment of the average person picked randomly off the street and thrust into a position of responsibility for the common good. In our skeptical and even cynical age, so often dominated by experts hired by the wealthy, this level of confidence in the potential of the common man for reasoned judgment seems misplaced. And yet it contributed significantly to one of the finest moments in the history of human culture and laid the groundwork for our present experiment in self-rule.

There were limits to the Greek view. As much as they venerated the ideal of a harmonious polity, they were no less divided by factionalism based on family loyalties, by the play of human ambition, and by the triumph of private over public interest, than any other community of flawed human beings. Citizenship to the classical Greeks, moreover, was confined only to men both of whose parents had been citizens. Women, slaves, and resident aliens (*metics*) were not qualified. Nor did Athenians believe in universal values or rights. Like the ancient Indians, another Indo-European people whose contacts with ancient Greece were not insignificant, they believed that privilege was a function of membership in a hereditary group. In addition, they also believed that democratic rule could be accomplished only on the small scale of a city-state where every citizen was allowed to participate personally. So in the Greek experience, as in our own contemporary world, democracy was not perfect. The same may be said of the Roman experiment.

Republican Rome

Roman institutions of self-governance developed at more or less the same time as did that of the Greeks and followed a different path. Around the year 500 BC the people of the city of Rome overthrew their king and instituted a form of government they called a 'republic,' derived from a combination of the Latin words *res*, meaning thing or affair, and *publicus*, meaning public. Government was thus 'an affair of the people.' This form of government lasted, through a number of permutations, until 27 BC when Octavian Augustus became emperor and initiated what historians refer to as the 'imperial' period, which lasted until the traditional date for the fall of the Roman empire in AD 476.

Here, as in Greece, it is important to note that the institutions of democratic governance arose not as a consequence of a sudden revelation that democracy is a superior form of government, but as a response to an eminently practical problem. In the late sixth century BC, the Roman community fell under the rule of a tyrant. The aristocratic families, who engineered his overthrow, understandably did not want to surrender their power to a new king but retain it for themselves. They adapted a venerable institution known as the Senate (deriving its name from *senex*, meaning 'old man'), which had hitherto functioned as a council of elders composed of representatives from each of the clans making up the state. The families now invested it with the responsibility of governing and gave it control over the budget.

Because the day-to-day administration of a complex state cannot be effectively undertaken by such a large group of people, the Roman aristocracy settled on a compromise in the form of two consuls who were elected for a period of only one year by a public assembly of citizens. Although this assembly was different from the Senate, the assembly was nevertheless controlled by the aristocratic families who dominated the Senate as well. The Romans thus built into their structure a system of checks and balances of a sort, and decreed that as one consul could exercise a veto over the decisions of the other. In such a case the Senate would have to resolve the difference. If an emergency of state arose calling for even more centralized decision-making, the Senate could appoint a 'dictator' whose term lasted only six months.

As time passed, the aristocratic families, who together formed a class known as the *patricians*, were gradually compelled to share power with the *plebians*, composed primarily of a class of free farmers. Once again, this broadening of participation in government did not come about as a consequence of democratic theory but as a practical compromise in a long struggle for power among the leading groups in Roman society. Throughout the period of the early republic in Rome (as well as in classical Greece), incidentally, governance remained patriarchal. Women played no overt role in politics.

After the Punic Wars between Rome and Carthage in the third and second centuries BC, Roman society changed significantly. First of all, vast numbers of slaves were imported into the Italian peninsula, which had the effect of creating huge landed estates in Italy on which the labor was done by slaves. The free farmers who had once formed the bedrock of Roman society were forced off the land, whence they migrated to Rome with nothing to do but amuse themselves in mindless entertainment of one form or another. Second, the empire itself grew over time from the peninsula of Italy to encompass the entire Mediterranean, raising challenges of governance that the republic had never faced before. The Romans granted citizenship to people spread throughout the eastern and western Mediterranean, but there was no mechanism for these citizens to participate in government, which was dominated by residents of the city of Rome.

From the perspective of hindsight, it is easy to see what should have happened. The *patrician* families who dominated Roman politics – together with the *plebians* who shared power with them – should have made the transition from direct democracy to representative democracy. That would have made it possible for the Roman government to scale upwards into ever larger units until the whole empire was included in a single form of representative government. Instead, only the city of Rome was democratic, and citizens had to come to the city to exercise their right to vote. Even there, unfortunately, the members of the aristocracy were usually unable to see beyond their immediate self-interest, and held on to power with a tenacity that ultimately destroyed the republic. As often happens in history, by trying to retain all their power they lost it all; had they been satisfied with less they would have retained more. The *plebians*, for their part, were composed of large numbers of poorly educated, unemployed, and easily aroused refugees from the countryside. They were easy prey for demagogues of every sort who played on the prejudices and fears of this urban rabble to gain power. By the first century BC the contest for power took increasingly violent form until finally civil wars broke out that ultimately threatened the survival of the state itself. In the face of impending anarchy, Octavian Augustus asserted firm control of the government by investing himself with the title of emperor. The republic was finished, a victim of its own failures of imagination and responsibility. There is some evidence, however, that the institution of the Senate continued to play a significant role in Roman politics well into the imperial period, providing a focal point for the expression of the popular will (particularly the interests of the aristocracy).[3]

The first experiments with representative bodies in the West actually took place in the Christian Church. There ecumenic councils, composed of representatives of churches throughout the eastern Mediterranean and north Africa, met to resolve disputes and clarify doctrine. The first was at Nicaea in 325 to deal with differing interpretations over the nature of Christ. The result was the statement of belief known as the Nicene Creed that remains basic to all three branches of Christianity: the Orthodox, Roman Catholic, and Protestant. The Church thereby contributed to the rise of democracy in the West not only in terms of representative institutions but also in terms of ideas, insofar as the Church continually stressed the inherent dignity of each individual created in the image of God. Later on, many of the fundamental tenets of popular sovereignty, as we shall see below, grew out of struggles between the Church and state in Western Europe. First, however, we should turn ourselves to the next landmark along the road, the Italian city-states.

Renaissance city-states in Italy

The Italian city-states occupied an important stage in the development of democratic institutions in the West. Beginning in the second half of the twelfth century, communities such as Padua, Milan, Florence, Pisa, Sienna, and Arezzo began to employ a new system of ruling councils, headed by chief executives known as *podestà*, who were granted both executive and judicial authority over the government. This new institution was a significant departure from the hitherto accepted norm of hereditary monarchy. The *podestà* was normally elected for a limited period – usually six months to a year – and was paid a fixed salary. He was obliged to consult with the council on all matters of substance. After stepping down he was subjected to a rigorous formal review of his conduct in office and in most cases was not allowed to serve in office for three years. Full sovereignty lay with the councils, composed of citizens themselves elected to office by residents of designated districts in the city who first met a number of broad criteria that included property ownership.

Another responsibility of the councils was to govern according to a written constitution of their own devising, and to alter the terms of that constitution when necessary according to a process that was open and inclusive. The councils typically consisted of about 600 members. These communities did not consider themselves 'democratic,' in part because the term was not brought into common use until William of Moerbeke used it in his translation of Aristotle's *Politics* in the middle of the thirteenth century.[4] In addition, many political philosophers in the late Middle Ages had adopted Aristotle's classification of good government as being represented by three institutional arrangements: monarchy, aristocracy, and polity, consisting, respectively, of government in the public interest by one, the few, and the many. Their respective corrupt forms were tyranny, oligarchy, and democracy, wherein those in power ruled in their own interest rather than the public interest. For them the term democracy implied what we might call 'mob rule.'

To be sure, these democratic institutions did not last long. The fatal flaw appears to have been a failure to open up access to power to those outside the control of an aristocracy determined to retain a hold on the position of *podestà*. Families who felt excluded formed factions that eventually undermined the solidarity of the polity. The struggles between those families, personified most famously by Shakespeare in *Romeo and Juliet*, created such chaos in the civil life of the cities that they were eventually compelled to hand over power to hereditary rulers such as the Medici in Florence and the Visconti in Milan. To be sure, not all cities lapsed back into monarchies. Venice, for example, retained a republican form of rule – though not its earlier dynamism – into the eighteenth century. But the legacy of these fascinating experiments in self-rule on later European history was more apparent in the realm of ideas than of institutions. They introduced two important concepts to European political thought: popular sovereignty and elective government.

In both cases Italian political philosophers tended to take their inspiration not so much from the Greek as from the Roman heritage. Perhaps that is not surprising, given that, as Italians, they often saw themselves as the natural heirs to the republican ideals of ancient Rome. One of their favorite sources was the Roman historian Sallust, who in his classic account of the *War with Cataline* argued that the underlying cause of Roman power and influence lay in the liberty of its early republic when

> at that time every man began to lift his head higher and to have his talents more in readiness. For kings hold the good in greater suspicion than the wicked, and to them the merit of others is always fraught with danger; still the free state, once liberty was won, waxed incredibly strong and great in a remarkably short time, such was the thirst for glory that had filled men's minds.[5]

The first major figure to raise the banner of popular sovereignty was Marsilius of Padua, whose *Defender of Peace*, published in 1324, is one of the landmarks on the long road to representative democracy. Marsilius wrote the work as an attack on the secular power of the Papacy, which based its claims on the priority of divine over human law. To counter that claim, Marsilius had to propose an alternative source of legitimacy, which he did in the agency of a general council that was the final authority not only for secular but for spiritual issues as well. He wrote that the power to legislate lies properly

> with the people or the whole body of citizens, or the weightier part thereof, through its election or will expressed by words in the general assembly of the citizens, commanding or determining that something be done or omitted with regard to human civil acts, under a temporal pain or punishment.[6]

In building their case for the importance of elective government, the Italian commentators argued that the institution of the monarchy was an obstacle to greatness. The most influential of them all in terms of impact on later thinkers was Niccolò Machiavelli. In the *Discourses* Machiavelli pointed out time and again the correlation between liberty and greatness in the experience of the Italian city-states. Arguing, following Sallust, that Rome was able to achieve greatness only after it had overthrown the monarchy, Machiavelli applied the same principle to his own time. He believed that only in a free republic where the citizens participated in self-government could the human potential be fully realized. Monarchy would not tolerate excellence. Any monarch worthy of the name would be more interested in preserving his own power than cultivating the talents of his subjects 'simply because, now wishing to have any cause to feel jealous of those over whom he is tyrannizing, he will find it impossible to give honorable employment to the best and most valiant citizens.'[7]

This posture by Machiavelli may come as a surprise to those whose only acquaintance with the Italian thinker is via *The Prince*, but it is important to keep in mind that in that work Machiavelli was trying to get his old job back by currying favor with the ruling Medicis in Florence. In the *Discourses*, however, he was more free to express his personal views on the superiority of a republic over a monarchy. In either case, Italy remained divided for 350 years after Machiavelli. Its weakness made it a playground for European power struggles, and the initiative in democratic thought and practice moved westward to Great Britain and then the United States.

England and the modern European experience

In England democratic institutions grew out of the struggle between parliament and the crown. Here the decentralized institutions of feudalism had grown up in the wake of the collapse of the Roman empire and in the absence of any strong centralized authority. Feudalism, though a highly complex institution that varied widely from place to place and time to time in Europe, centered around a contractual relationship between a lord and his vassals. In this arrangement a given lord promised his vassals title to their land in return for their promise of military service to him. The system was hierarchical, creating a pyramidal structure in which each lord had his own vassals but himself served as a vassal to a higher lord. The highest lord of all was the king, and the association of his vassals in time developed into the institution of parliament.

Meanwhile, the monarchs of Europe began to consolidate and then expand their power both internally and externally in the fourteenth and fifteenth centuries, thereby coming into increasing conflict with each other. The ensuing centuries of warfare led, very gradually and with much twisting and turning along the way, to the rise of the modern nation-state. In that process monarchs sought to neutralize the power of the aristocracy (and of the Church) in order to enhance their own power. In France, for example, Louis XIV struck a deal with the nobility in which he absolved them from paying taxes in return for their loyalty to the monarchy. Each paid a price for that deal. The nobility were in essence emasculated. By surrendering their obligation to pay taxes they unwittingly also gave up the only bargaining chip they had over the monarch: the threat to withhold taxes. For his part, Louis gained power in the short run but lost a valuable source of revenue, eventually undermining the financial viability of the state.

In England the aristocracy retained their obligation to pay taxes, and over time used the threat of withholding taxes to their advantage in gaining ever greater power for parliament. By the end of the eighteenth century Britain was well on its way to becoming a constitutional monarchy in which real power lay in the representative institution of the parliament. Many commentators of the time saw the British system of government as a representation of Aristotle's mixed government, combining the best of monarchy, aristocracy, and democracy in the respective institutions of the king, the House of Lords, and the House of Commons. Whether Britain qualifies to be called a 'democracy' at that point in its development hinges on the extent of the suffrage, which was strictly limited to the aristocracy.

The first country to cross the line into a full-fledged democracy in the modern world was probably the United States, which declared its independence from Great Britain in 1776. By doing so Americans effectively eliminated the institution of the monarchy, as well as that of the aristocracy, from the mix of governmental institutions and replaced them with the concept of a citizenry free and equal in all respects. The distinguished American historian Gordon Wood has written that the American Revolution 'made Americans (despite the contradictory persistence of slavery until the middle decades of the nineteenth century) the first people in the modern world to possess a truly democratic government and society.'[8]

For the first few generations of the new republic's existence, the term 'democracy' still tended to be used in its Aristotelian sense, that is, as a derogatory term implying mob rule. The more acceptable term was 'republic,' which was supposed to connote a rejection of monarchy and the opening of political representation beyond the bounds of the aristocracy but still confined to those most inclined to have the leisure to pursue virtue, the income to put them beyond the reach of private interests, and the responsibility that comes from management of estates, i.e., the landed gentry.

This view of government, however, did not appeal to the vast majority of the population in the young country. The ideal of equality, together with the widespread belief that one group, no matter how enlightened, could not be expected to look after the often conflicting interests of all the disparate communities, eventually undermined the elitist assumptions of the founding generation. By the third decade of the nineteenth century, most of the states had passed legislation granting suffrage to all adult white males. This American innovation, moreover, didn't stop at expanding the suffrage. It also expanded access to public office as well. Although George Washington, the quintessential representative of the traditional outlook of the gentry farmer serving his country, refused to accept a salary during his years of public service, all representatives to the Congress were paid a salary from the beginning in order to make it possible for those who were not wealthy to accept political office. To get some idea of how unique this was, members of parliament in Great Britain were not paid a salary until 1911. By opening up public service to all, one of the most visible marks of class distinction was removed.

Wider suffrage thus had the effect of bringing into public office people who had no pretence to aristocracy. Any hint of membership in aristocratic circles, in fact, became a handicap. The quintessential symbol of this new openness in American democracy was Andrew Jackson, who swept into the presidency in the election of 1828 as a representative of the common man. Jackson, who once remarked that he had no respect for someone who could think of only one way to spell a word, was capable of appealing to a mass audience as no politician before him had even tried to do. A new age in American democracy opened up, putting into practice ideals of equality that political observers in the past had talked about but never implemented.

Democratic governance on the European continent during the late eighteenth century and then throughout the nineteenth century had much more shallow roots. It was in France that the ideal of freedom and equality seemed at first to have so much promise. In 1789 French revolutionaries overthrew the monarchy of Louis XIV and established a republic committed to the goals of '*liberté, égalité,* and *fraternité.*' Though France soon relapsed into an even more centralized and oppressive monarchy under Napoleon than the one it had just overthrown, it is hard to exaggerate the impact of the French Revolution on the imagination of idealistic European intellectuals, and then, in the twentieth century, on freedom-loving revolutionaries throughout the colonial world of Asia and Africa. Some historians have noted that the three main ideologies, or 'isms,' of the last two centuries – liberalism, socialism, and nationalism, were descendants of the rallying cry of the French Revolution mentioned above: liberty, equality, and brotherhood. In any event, the French people had a strong tendency, noted by Tocqueville in *The Old Regime and the French Revolution*, to sacrifice freedom on the altar of equality.

By eliminating all the institutional remnants of the traditional order – the aristocracy, the Church, the regional parliaments, the autonomous cities, among others – all in the name of equality, the French people essentially cleared the decks of all obstacles to the centralization of political power into the hands of the tyrant Napoleon. French democracy, as a result, took much longer to mature, and many argue that the animosities between the working and the middle classes that were ignited during the French Revolution have continued to influence politics in France even down to the present. The English, on the other hand, by retaining their traditional pluralistic institutions such as the aristocracy, had used those very institutions to expand their liberties at the expense of the monarch, in the process reaching a much more stable balance of freedom and equality without which democracy cannot survive.

The situation in Germany was scarcely better. There too nationalism tended to trump liberalism. The fact that Germany was not fully unified until the middle of the nineteenth century, and then by a militaristic government that gave the appearance of constitutional rule while retaining all power in the hands of the monarch, prevented democracy from being born until after the First World War. Even then, under the ill-fated Weimar period, it died when Hitler took over the reins of power in 1933. Only after the Second World War, and then only in West Germany, did stable democracy finally come to the German people. In Eastern Europe, as well as in Spain and Italy, democracy existed only in the hopes of generations of idealistic intellectuals until after the collapse of the Soviet Union. Only in Scandinavia did democracy become a reality in the nineteenth century, and then thrive in the twentieth.

This checkered history of democracy, even in Europe, is useful to keep in mind as we now turn our attention to Asia. The democratic prerequisites – such as pluralistic institutions capable of limiting the power of a central ruler and conditions of peace and stability – come in remarkably varied configurations. And democracy, once won, can be lost.

Notes

1 M.I. Finley, *Democracy Ancient and Modern* (London: The Hogarth Press, 1985), p. 23.
2 Thucydides, trans. Rex Warner, *History of the Peloponnesian War* (New York: Penguin, 1972). This speech, together with Lincoln's Gettysburg Address and his second inaugural speech, were the first places I went for consolation and understanding after the attack on the World Trade Center on September 11, 2001.

3 The scholar who has championed this view is Professor Fergus Millar. See *The Roman Republic and the Augustan Revolution* (Chapel Hill: University of North Carolina Press, 2002).
4 Quentin Skinner, 'The Italian City-Republics,' in *Democracy: The Unfinished Journey*, edited by John Dunn (New York: Oxford University Press, 1992), p. 59.
5 *Sallust*, trans. by J.C. Rolfe (Cambridge, MA: Harvard University Press, 1921), pp. 13–15.
6 Quoted in Quentin Skinner, p. 62.
7 From the second book of the *Discourses*, quoted in Quentin Skinner, 'The Italian City-Republics,' in *Democracy: The Unfinished Journey*, ed. John Dunn (New York: Oxford University Press, 1992), p. 67.
8 Gordon S. Wood, 'Democracy and the American Revolution,' in *Democracy: The Unfinished Journey*, ed. John Dunn (New York: Oxford University Press, 1992), p. 91.

Further reading

There is a huge and rapidly growing body of literature on democracy. What follows is just a beginning, a tantalizing antipasto. For a classic, clearly written treatment of Western political thought, consult any of the editions of George Sabine's *A History of Political Theory*. An extremely helpful collection of essays on the evolution of democratic institutions in the West is contained in *Democracy: The Unfinished Journey 508 BC to AD 1993*, edited by John Dunn (New York: Oxford University Press, 1992). Donald W. Treadgold's *Freedom: A History* (New York: New York University Press, 1990) is a history of free political institutions that is global in scope. *Education for Democracy: Citizenship, Community, Service: A Sourcebook for Students and Teachers*, edited by Benjamin Barber and Richard M. Battistoni (Dubuque: Kendall/Hunt Publishing, 1993), is an excellent collection of readings on the general subject of American democracy, as is Stephen John Goodlad's *The Last Best Hope: A Democracy Reader* (San Francisco: Jossey-Bass, 2001). A well-written discussion of Athenian democracy can be found in *The Honey and the Hemlock: Democracy and Paranoia in Ancient Athens and Modern America* (New York: Basic Books, 1991). M.I. Finley's *Democracy Ancient and Modern* (London: The Hogarth Press, 1985) is a delightful and clearly written discussion of the relevance of Greek democracy to the modern world, especially in terms of the need for greater public participation in politics. For insightful discussions on democracy in a global perspective, see Steven Muhlberger and Phil Paine, 'Democracy's Place in World History,' *Journal of World History* 4 (Spring 1993), pp. 23–45; and Ron Bontekoe and Marietta Stepaniants, eds, *Justice and Democracy: Cross-Cultural Perspectives* (Honolulu: University of Hawai'i Press, 1997). Other treatments of the Greek experience include A.H.M. Jones, *Athenian Democracy* (Baltimore: Johns Hopkins University Press, 1986); and David Stockton, *The Classical Athenian Democracy* (New York: Oxford University Press, 1990). Philip Green's *Democracy* (New York: Prometheus, 1993); and Arend Lijphart's *Democracy in Plural Societies* (New Haven: Yale University Press, 1980) are also useful introductions. Of course the classic work on American democracy is Alexis de Tocqueville's *Democracy in America*, published first in 1835–1840, now available in many editions.

Chapter 3

Post-war democracies in Asia
India, Japan, and the Philippines

In this chapter we consider three very different examples of Asian democracy that emerged immediately after the Second World War: India in South Asia, Japan in East Asia, and the Philippines in Southeast Asia. In India, democratic institutions were adopted from the beginning of the country's emergence from British colonialism as an independent state in 1947. In Japan, democratic institutions were in part a consequence of willingly retaining a constitution originally imposed on the Japanese by the American occupation in the years between the defeat of Japan in 1945 and the return of its full sovereignty in April 1952. In the Philippines, democracy was also instituted as a result of American influence, in this case when the independence of the Republic of the Philippines was declared on July 4, 1946, ending almost half a century of American rule.

In spite of wide differences in cultural and historical experience, the people of these three countries have demonstrated a remarkable commitment to the principles of democratic governance. In two of them – India and the Philippines – government for a time fell into the hands of leaders who usurped power but who were eventually displaced by a resurgence of popular rule. Their stories illustrate both the tenaciousness of democratic practices once they have taken root in a country's experience and the dangers to democracy that may arise from the temptation by popularly elected officials to abuse power. The story of democracy in India, Japan, and the Philippines is part inspiration, part warning.

India
History

For many Westerners the first image that India evokes is the Taj Mahal, built by the Mughal emperor Shah Jahan as a tomb for his beloved wife Mumtaz Mahal in the middle of the seventeenth century. In many ways the Taj is entirely appropriate as a symbol of India (in spite of being an Islamic mosque in a country inhabited mostly by Hindus). First of all, it is a religious monument in a culture where the spiritual dimension has played a central role throughout its history. Second, in a country marked by ethnic and linguistic diversity of breathtaking proportions, the Taj is a sublime expression of the human capacity for creative synthesis. It combines elements of Arabic, Persian, and Hindu architecture into a unified whole of unsurpassed beauty and grace.

The challenge faced by the architect of the Taj is the challenge of modern India — to forge unity out of diversity while retaining a healthy balance between the need for central constraints and the need for local freedom. The scope of the challenge is immense. The seventh-largest country in the world in terms of area, India is the second-largest in terms of population. With over one billion people, it constitutes approximately one-sixth of the world's total population.

The history of India originates in the Indus Valley civilization in the third millennium BC. Its location and topography have rendered it vulnerable to invasion from the outside from early times to the present. This frequent intercourse with foreign influences has stimulated the creative imagination of the Indian peoples in all forms of the arts and literature and philosophy as well as science and technology and basic political and social institutions. For most of its history, whatever unity India possessed was usually religious, social, economic, and cultural rather than political. There were two exceptions: the Mauryan empire under the great ruler Ashoka in the third century BC, and the Gupta dynasty in the fourth and fifth centuries AD. Afterward India was dominated by regional kingdoms until the ascendancy of the Mughal empire in the sixteenth century. Even then rule was never extended into all of southern India until the conquest of India by the British in the eighteenth century. For a time India was governed as a satrapy of the British East India Company until the British crown took over in 1858, at which point India became a formal part of the British empire controlled from London.

It is very difficult if not impossible to generalize about a country as large and diverse as India, calling to mind the observation made by Indians themselves that whatever generalization one makes about India, its opposite is also true. Nevertheless, there are some patterns that appear often enough to be worthy of mention. One is a tradition of government by discussion that goes far back to early India. Indeed, there is some reason to believe that early India enjoyed democratic institutions comparable to those developed in Greece. In the period from about 600 BC to AD 200, India consisted of republics, in many of which there existed a form of political participation that was eventually adopted by the Buddhist monastic institutions, whose affairs were governed by periodic meetings of the monks themselves. The Buddha himself, who lived during this period and whose father presided over one such republic whose policies were regularly discussed in an assembly, has been called by one of the greatest historians of India 'an apostle of democracy.'[1] Village councils, known as *panchayat* (mentioned in the introduction) were typically composed of elected representatives with rather wide executive and judicial powers, including the responsibility for distributing land and collecting taxes. At some point in the past women served on this body, but that did not last until modern times. In the 1990s, the government of India has mandated that women once again serve on local village councils.

This tradition of local self-government formed a chain of continuity in rural India that lasted through many periods of conquest by outsiders, including the British. It was an acknowledgement of the value of local rule in a country as vast as India. In the words of one of the early classics from the tenth century, 'public opinion is more powerful than the king as the rope made of many fibres is strong enough to drag a lion.'[2] On the level of the central government, the British only very gradually began to include Indians in the decision-making bodies of government. By the 1830s Indians had begun to be included in offices formerly open only to British citizens. In accordance with the Indian Councils Act of 1861, Indian leaders were brought into the deliberations of the Executive Council, which was responsible for the highest level of policy decisions. A paradox arose with respect to the British treatment of Indian intellectuals. Intending to make Indian nationals effective servants of British rule, the British government encouraged educated Indians to send their children to schools and universities in Britain, as well as in Indian cities such as Bombay, Calcutta, and Madras where education was modeled on the British curriculum. There they absorbed not only the lessons of British administration but also the ideals of popular sovereignty and freedom that permeated European political thought. Small wonder that when they applied those principles to India they found much to be desired. The British were later to discover that they had in effect sown the seeds of their own expulsion from the Indian subcontinent. In the process, however, they had also done a better job of any of the other European colonial powers in preparing their colonies for eventual independence.

One of the early milestones on the long road to democratic governance in India was the founding of the Indian National Congress in 1885. Composed of leaders of the growing body of British-educated elite in India, this party soon became the catalyst for the independence movement in India. Its prestige was such that after independence in 1947 it constituted the major party of Indian politics for the second half of the twentieth century. By 1905 it was calling for Indian self-government. The First World War represented another step forward for Indian political self-consciousness. Upwards of three-quarters of a million Indian soldiers served the war in Europe, the Middle East, and Africa. Almost forty thousand were killed. In partial recognition of their contribution to the war effort, the British government passed the Government of India Act in 1919 granting increased participation to Indians in the administration of government, including greater opportunities for service in the civil service and military officer corps.

By 1920 leadership of the Indian independence movement was assumed by an Indian lawyer trained in London and with experience organizing against British policies in South Africa: Mohandas K. Gandhi. Drawing on the spiritual heritage of more than one of the great Indian religions, Gandhi developed a policy of non-violent civil disobedience against British rule that brought gradual reforms to the structure of government in India during the 1930s. Nevertheless, until the Second World War transformed the political landscape of the world, ending European dominance of the global arena that had prevailed for centuries, the British government continued to resist Indian demands for complete independence.

During the war the gap between the Hindu and Muslim communities in India widened. Convinced that the Congress Party did not represent Muslim interests, Muhammad Ali Jinnah, the leader of the Muslim League, began to agitate for a separate state of Pakistan for Muslims. After the war, confronted with increasing violence between the Muslim and Hindu communities in India, the British government granted independence to India on August 15, 1947. Simultaneously, they created the new state of Pakistan out of territory on the eastern portion of India (which became Bangladesh in 1971) and the western portion (which was known as West Pakistan until 1971 and thereafter simply as Pakistan).

The constitution of India was adopted in 1950, creating a parliamentary form of government modeled in part on the British system but containing elements that are also more applicable to the Indian context. A great deal of credit for the success of the democratic experiment in India goes to its first prime minister, Jawaharlal Nehru, who became the most important political figure in India after the assassination of Mahatma Gandhi in 1948.

There are moments in the life of an institution where the accident of personality plays a crucial role. Just such an accident took place in post-independence India in the person of Nehru. Whatever errors of judgment he may have made in the realm of economic development by favoring a planned socialist economy, it was Nehru's abiding commitment to democracy that is his greatest legacy to India. There were many moments in the early years when provincial governments or members of the judicial branch acted contrary to Nehru's wishes. A statesman of a lesser order might have taken advantage of the plasticity of these new institutions to subvert their authority. Nehru did not. As a result, habits of self-government and judicial independence were allowed to take root and flourish.

When Nehru died in 1964, he was succeeded as prime minister by Lal Bahadur Shastri, a long-time Congress Party leader. During Shastri's time in office India and Pakistan went to war over Kashmir, and were finally prevailed upon to stop the conflict only after they had fought each other to a stalemate. When Shastri died of a heart attack in 1966, Nehru's daughter, Indira Gandhi (no relation to Mahatma Gandhi) was named head of the Congress Party and prime minister. After consolidating her power she also confronted war with Pakistan, this time over the efforts of East Pakistan to sue for independence as Bangladesh. After defeating the Pakistani army handily in a matter of weeks in 1971, Indira then went on to underscore Indian military power by detonating India's first nuclear weapon in 1974.

When the oil crisis of 1974 severely hurt the Indian economy, her standing in the country fell precipitously. Under threat by the courts for election tampering, she declared a state of emergency in 1975, imprisoning her political opponents and clamping a lid on the country's normally free press. After two years of economic improvement, she felt confident enough in 1977 to call for national elections. She lost decisively. The episode underlined both the vulnerability and the resilience of Indian democracy.

Morarji Desai was named prime minister, but was ineffective in power and alienated the populace by prosecuting Indira for crimes that did not hold up in court. The result was that national elections in 1980 brought Indira back into power. Her own rule ended in tragedy in 1984 when she was assassinated by one of her Sikh guards who had been radicalized by Indira's violent repression of Sikh extremists demanding an independent Sikh state in the Punjab.

Rajiv Gandhi, Indira's son and Nehru's grandson, was promptly elected to replace her as prime minister in 1984. Troubled by internal crises, including numerous corruption scandals, and lacking the political instincts and experience of his mother and grandfather, Rajiv was voted out of office in 1989. In 1991, while campaigning for reelection, Rajiv was assassinated by a terrorist supporting the Tamil uprising in Sri Lanka (which Rajiv had sent Indian troops to help suppress in 1987). P.V. Narasimha Rao became prime minister in 1991 and embarked on an ambitious program to replace the centralized socialist economy built by Nehru with a market-oriented system free of stifling government controls. In his five years in office some progress was made but much remained to be done. The late 1990s were a time of considerable uncertainty, during which the Congress Party seemed unable to clean house and rid itself of corruption at the highest levels. Most troubling was the rise of the Bharatiya Janata Party (BJP), whose extreme Hindu nationalism threatened to spark communal conflict with the Muslim minority. The quality of leadership in Indian politics seemed to be in short supply even as the country began to prosper economically as never before.

Institutions

India's constitution draws primarily from the British tradition but also incorporates elements from the United States. Like the British system, it is a parliamentary democracy with two legislative houses: a lower house known as the Lok Sabha in which all representatives are elected directly by universal adult suffrage. They represent the twenty-eight states of India in numbers that are directly proportional to the size of the population in each state. The other house, known as the Rajya Sabha, consists of members elected by the legislative assemblies of the various states. The term of office is five years for the Lok Sabha, six years for the Rajya Sabha. Like the American system, the Indian government is divided into three branches: executive, legislative, and judicial, with safeguards designed to insure a measure of autonomy of each branch from interference by either of the other two. Also like the American system, the structure of government in India is federalist, with strong state legislatures that reflect the diverse cultural identities of their populations.

Elections in India are free, fair, and often frequent. On numerous occasions in six decades of democratic government in India, elections have overturned the party in power and substituted the opposition. Another one of the institutional bulwarks of Indian democracy is freedom of expression and access to alternative sources of information. Except during the period of Indira Gandhi's emergency in the mid-1970s, there have been few limits on the free expression of ideas in India. Radio and television stations were once owned by the government but are now open to private competition. The increased availability of programs via satellite has considerably widened access to information from outside the country, as has the Internet. Its press is by all accounts free and aggressive in criticizing the self-serving antics of government officials and politicians. Newspapers in India, of which there are more than 30,000 in the country as a whole, are private and operate without government control.

To be sure, a large sector of the population is unable to read the newspapers, for the simple reason that almost half the Indian population is illiterate. Indeed, one of the fascinating peculiarities of Indian democracy is the widespread illiteracy of the electorate, making it unlikely they will be able to follow the nuances of public policy, or participate in their conception and execution, with any degree of sophistication. But Indian democracy, in spite of this handicap, has been widely successful, appearing to vindicate the broader conception of democracy associated in the American experience with Andrew Jackson. Jacksonian democracy cast its electoral net to include the entire adult population (with, of course, notable exceptions such as women and blacks) regardless of education or economic status. In this respect, both the American and Indian experiments in democracy share a similar faith in the ability of the common citizen to form reliable judgments about politics.

The opportunities for Indians to form political associations free of governmental control are widespread. Although the Congress Party dominated Indian politics for decades after independence in 1947, increasing complacency and corruption (as noted above) have so damaged its public reputation that it lost control of parliament in the mid-1990s. It remains to be seen whether Congress leaders can clear out the deadwood sufficiently to renew their mandate to rule. There are many regional parties that dominate specific states but have no national standing, which also contribute to the diversity of institutions representing different points of view. Some have argued that the disintegration of the Congress Party has led to a devolution of power from the center and the rise of groups that focus on local and regional interests at the expense of the public good. One scholar, for example, has written that

> although India is blessed with a robust civil society and a rich and vigorous associational life, the patterns of associationism usually correlate to the narrow caste, ethnic, regional, and communal chauvinisms, including patriarchy, class domination, and other tyrannies, which have deep roots in civil society.[3]

The issue of inclusivity, which Robert Dahl regards as essential to an effective democracy, is very interesting in the Indian context. From the very beginning of the republic's existence after independence, prime minister Nehru was committed to the inclusion of all groups, once remarking that

> the caste system and much that goes with it are wholly incompatible, reactionary, restrictive, and barriers to progress. There can be no equality in status and opportunity within its framework, nor can there be political democracy and much less economic democracy.[4]

The government has accordingly supported a variety of affirmative action programs designed to insure that formerly excluded groups in Indian society be granted opportunities for education and public service. Women vote along with men, and the percentage of women who vote in elections is now almost equal to that of the men, which is at an admirable rate of almost 60 percent.

Conditions

The essential conditions for democracy in India are in general very favorable. In significant contrast to Pakistan, the military and the police have been largely subordinate to the elected politicians since the beginning of the Indian republic in 1947. After more than half a century, that tradition seems firmly in place and is not likely to change. Democratic beliefs and a political culture deeply supportive of democracy have been characteristic of Indian politics from the beginning of Indian independence and remain very strong. Tested during the emergency declared by Indira Gandhi in the 1970s, they have become if anything stronger as the years pass. India from the time of independence has moreover enjoyed complete sovereignty and is not subject to the control of any foreign state.

That is not to say that Indian democracy does not face severe challenges. There are three unfavorable conditions: an economy choked by a long heritage of bureaucratic interference, an intolerable level of corruption particularly in the Congress Party, and a diversity of ethnic, caste, regional, and religious groupings that make coherent policy-making difficult. The first challenge is a consequence of Nehru's commitment to a centrally planned, socialist economy modeled on the Soviet command economy. Only in the early 1990s did the government begin a process of opening the Indian economy to global market forces and reducing government interference. The second challenge, corruption, is a consequence of the Congress Party having stayed in power too long, exposing its leaders to the inevitable temptations to line their own pockets with the public's money. The third challenge — the breathtaking heterogeneity of the Indian sub-continent — is both a strength and a weakness. On the one hand the multiple communities that make up the nation act as a natural check on central power. On the other hand, they set in place a culture of competition and distrust that inhibits cooperation for the common good. Parties such as the Bharatya Janata (BJP) exploit populist ideologies such as Hindu nationalism to build support for themselves, alienating sectors of the voting public of different ethnicities, and diverting the terms of public debate from more substantive issues of policy.

A balanced assessment of something so complex as democracy in India is not easy. Perhaps the best approach is to identify its triumphs and failures, as well as its challenges for the future. Its greatest achievement may have been its ability to prevent mass starvation. Famine in India was endemic during the years of British rule, and given the tripling of the Indian population since independence one might have expected famines to increase. Yet there has never been a serious famine in independent India. The presence of opposition parties and a free press has made the government far more responsive to local needs than it ever was under colonial or autocratic rule. One has only to contemplate the experience of China to appreciate the magnitude of this difference. There 30 million peasants died of starvation in the late 1950s and early 1960s — by far the greatest famine anywhere in the world at any time in history — as a direct result of Mao Zedong's failed Great Leap Forward. Indeed, this ability to prevent famine may be one of democracy's greatest contributions. The Nobel Prize-winning economist Amartya Sen has written that 'no famine has ever taken place in the history of the world in a functioning democracy — be it economically rich (as in contemporary Western Europe or North America) or relatively poor (as in postindependence India, or Botswana, or Zimbabwe).'[5] In many other areas as well India has made remarkable progress. Its infant mortality has been reduced from 146 per thousand at independence to 68 in 1995, its life expectancy raised from 32 to 62, its GNP per capita increased from $60 to $340, its illiteracy reduced from 82 percent to 48 percent.

Much remains to be done. Although many economies in East and Southeast Asia started out at roughly the same point in the late 1940s, their progress has been dramatically faster than India's. Its greatest failure has been to reduce the gap between the rich and the poor. The number of people living in poverty in India today – almost one-third of the population – is almost equal to the total population of India in 1947. Illiteracy remains unacceptably high. The greatest argument for optimism is probably that India is now beginning to undertake the reforms necessary to confront these challenges successfully.

Japan

History

Modern Japan is a study in contrasts. With no natural resources to speak of, it is now the world's second largest economy. With a language and culture that are distinctly different from its neighbors, it has nevertheless borrowed extensively from Korea and China over the millennia. After a period of deliberate isolation from the outside world during the Tokugawa period from 1600 to 1868, it modernized rapidly in the last three decades of the nineteenth century and was able to maintain its sovereignty during the golden age of European colonialism in the decades leading up to the First World War. Although the emperor in Japan is one of the most important institutions in modern Japanese history, he has no real power.

These contrasts form the warp and woof of traditional as well as modern Japanese history. Japan emerged into its literate, historical phase relatively late, having adopted the Chinese script for its first writing system only in the late fifth century AD. The period from then until the tenth century witnessed considerable Chinese influence in terms of Confucian ideology and Chinese art and politics. From the tenth century until about 1600 Japan passed through a period of decentralized rule by local warriors known as *samurai*. There are some parallels between the Japanese system and European feudalism, though the Japanese based their relationships more on personal loyalty and blood ties than legal contract, as did the Europeans. In 1600 Japan was brought together under a more centralized form of rule by Tokugawa Ieyasu, whose descendants ruled as shoguns from Edo (now Tokyo) until they were overthrown in 1868.

The Meiji Restoration, as the period of reform was called in the nineteenth century, adopted a political constitution modeled on Prussia. The legislature, known as the Diet, was responsible to the emperor, not the people. But since the emperor had no power, the actual decisions were made by a group of advisers who engineered sweeping reforms in all aspects of Japanese life. They adopted a modern legal code that abolished all *samurai* privileges, completely reformed the educational system, instituted a commercial code based on the French model, established a modern financial structure, and built a brand-new infrastructure in transportation and communication that changed dramatically the daily lives of the average Japanese. Manifesting many of the same characteristics associated with the modernization of Germany, the reforms were implemented in the name of the state (embodied in the person of the emperor). In the space of little more than one generation, Japan had changed from a traditional autocracy to a modern constitutional government. It was a remarkable transformation.

In 1912 a conflict within the government between the military and the main political party in Japan over funding priorities led to a political crisis between various factions in the Diet. Out of the ensuing struggle emerged another political party that gave Japan a two-party system which lasted until 1932. In other respects as well Japan's democratic institutions were strengthened in the first few decades of the twentieth century. One of the most positive developments in this period, known as the era of Taisho democracy after the name of the emperor who reigned at the time, was the passage of universal male suffrage in 1925, increasing the number of voters from 3 to almost 12 million. By the end of the 1920s, however, a combination of factors exacerbated by the world-wide depression undermined public confidence in democratic institutions. When the prime minister of Japan was assassinated by right-wing fanatics in 1932, the government fell under the control of militarists who essentially usurped power in the name of the emperor. They then proceeded to set Japan on a course of imperialism in China that eventually provoked war first with China in 1937 and then with the United States in 1941. In 1945, soon after the Americans dropped atomic bombs on Hiroshima and Nagasaki, Japan surrendered. For the first time in Japanese history the country was occupied by foreign troops (under the command of the American General Douglas MacArthur).

The American occupation, which lasted from 1945 until 1952, when full sovereignty was restored to Japan, was a period of democratic reform. After several attempts to get Japanese leaders to write a draft constitution that placed sovereignty in the hands of the people instead of the emperor, MacArthur finally ordered his own staff to produce a draft constitution in February 1946, giving them only a week to produce a draft. That constitution has remained in effect in Japan ever since. It made the executive branch – the Cabinet – responsible to parliament, not the emperor, and included a bill of rights similar to that contained in the American constitution. Other democratic reforms were instituted as well. Women were granted the right to vote, and eligibility to vote was reduced from age 25 to 20. For many years after the war, the preponderance of scholarly opinion gave primary credit for the subsequent success of Japanese democracy to the American occupation. That view has now changed to one that assigns a much greater role to the institutions of pre-war democracy which had evolved in Japan during the early years of the twentieth century.

For almost forty years after full sovereignty was restored to Japan, from 1955 to 1993, the conservative Liberal Democratic Party (LDP) controlled the government in Japan. Opposition parties, of which the most significant were communist and socialist, were unable to cooperate sufficiently to oust the LDP. LDP support in the electorate was based on Japan's miraculous economic recovery from the rubble of the Second World War to the third-largest economy in the world by 1970, behind only the United States and the Soviet Union. Under these conditions of rapid growth, the LDP was able to command public confidence to stay in power. In 1993, the LDP was voted out of office, but only for a short period. By 1996 they were back in power, and remained there until at least 2003, in spite of repeated hopes for an effective opposition movement within the Japanese political system.

Institutions

The practical significance of the institutional structure of Japanese democracy is not fully apparent by describing the bare bones of the structure itself, calling to mind the observation that a wolf and a dog are structurally the same, but react very differently to a pat on the head. The electoral system in Japan is a case in point. For most of post-war Japanese history, election to the Diet was based upon proportional representation. The underlying principle of proportional representation, which is more common in continental Europe than Britain and North America, is that the political makeup of the legislature will mirror the full spectrum of political views in the general public. Championed first by nineteenth-century thinkers such as John Stuart Mill who were fearful of the tyranny of the majority, the benefit of this system, which results in multi-party legislatures rather than two-party legislatures, is that minority views have a forum for expression. The weakness of the system, however, is that too often nothing gets done in the absence of a clear consensus. In Japan the weakness is far more in evidence than the strength.

The Japanese constitution added its own peculiar twist by creating districts with more than one Diet representative. Since some districts had as many as six representatives, and since political parties routinely fielded several candidates for election in the same district, campaigns tended to be about personalities rather than about issues. Campaigns also tended to be about money, since candidates enhanced their public standing by providing expensive services to their constituencies. To raise the money necessary to win elections, candidates had to join a faction within the Liberal Democratic Party (LDP), which would then help finance their campaigns. The leaders of those factions, in turn, raised money from businesses and organizations who were thankful for governmental policies (instituted by the LDP) that favored their interests. If that sounds like a cozy, and potentially corrupting, relationship between politics and business, it was.

In 1993, when (as noted above) the LDP was voted out of office for the first time since 1955, the electoral system was reformed. Multi-member districts were abolished and limits were set for campaign contributions. In addition, the total number of Diet representatives was reduced from 512 to 500 (300 from districts and 200 selected by a system of proportional representation). It is too early to tell whether these reforms will have their intended effect. The Japanese government has been notably slow on many fronts to respond effectively to the need for additional reforms. Many foreign observers believe that the Japanese propensity for collective action undermines the sense of individual responsibility required for effective leadership in times of crisis.[6] Meanwhile, public confidence in politicians seems to be eroding in the absence of strong leadership.

On another front, Japanese democracy is buttressed by a free press with very high standards. Japanese newspapers are widely revered for their quality and integrity. Their major newspapers, of which the most widely regarded is probably the *Asahi Shimbun*, have circulations in the millions and are national in their distribution. The major drawback of the Japanese press is that their reporters have a cozier relationship with government bureaucrats and politicians than in many other democracies. Nevertheless, they can be tenacious in their criticism of the government. Book and magazine publishing is open and widely influential in Japan, a nation of avid readers.

It goes without saying that the freedom to associate in political groups is not limited to any significant extent in Japan, other than what would be necessary to promote public security. Groups of all kinds are allowed to organize and distribute literature. What does represent a challenge both to Japanese democracy and beyond to Japanese society in general is the issue of inclusive citizenship. The Japanese have traditionally taken pride in their cultural homogeneity. As an island nation, they have been less vulnerable than the Chinese or Koreans to invasions from outside forces, and this simple fact of geography has encouraged an insular mentality toward the outside world. While homogeneity has many advantages in terms of democratic governance, insofar as it enhances cooperation and trust, in the case of Japan it also has serious flaws.

The biggest problem is demographic. Japan is facing the same general decline in population that all developed countries are experiencing. The difference is that in Europe and the United States, governments are willing to import labor by relaxing immigration barriers. Japan, in part because of its cultural isolation and in part because of government policy, has so far been unable to do so. The demographic prospects in Japan are sobering. For years the rate of population growth has fallen below replacement. If current trends continue, the population will peak at about 128 million in 2007 and then begin to fall rapidly to about 120 million in 2025 and then to 101 million in 2050. In the year 2000 there were four workers supporting every retired person; by the year 2025 there will be only 2.2 workers supporting every retired person.[7] When Japan faced such a labor crunch in the past, they imported hundreds of thousands of laborers from their colony in Korea. But to this day the descendants of those Koreans have been denied citizenship in Japan and face institutional discrimination of all kinds. In terms of inclusivity, therefore, Japanese democracy has a long way to go.

Conditions

The essential conditions for the growth of democracy in Japan are all positive. After the Second World War, neither the military nor the police have played any role whatsoever in Japanese politics. Democracy in Japan now has a heritage of almost fifty years to draw on, including a brief moment in the mid-1990s when the dominant party of Liberal Democrats was voted out of office. There is no question that the people support democracy and wish to continue it. In addition, there is no strong foreign power hostile to democracy who controls Japanese affairs. After the American occupation ended in 1952 Japan has been a fully sovereign state in every way. Japan also has favorable conditions for the survival of its strong democracy. The economy, though it has passed through a ten-year slump of historic proportions in the 1990s, is the second-largest economy in the world, oriented to the global market economy and open to the outside world. It has a homogeneous society to a fault, as I have mentioned above.

This is not to say, however, that Japanese democracy is not without challenges. The pillars of Japanese society are the civil bureaucracy of the central government, parliament, and business. Convinced that only they know what is in Japan's interests, they manipulate the levers of power in Japan by cooperating with each other and by ignoring the wishes of the Japanese people. During the years of economic growth from the 1950s to the 1980s, nobody complained. Since then, however, times have changed but that core troika of institutions have not. They remain committed to what writer Karel van Wolferen has called 'bureaucratic authoritarianism.'[8] Because Japanese institutions are based upon consensus and not strong individual leadership, and because the consensus-makers are not inclined to favor reforms that would undermine their own power, Japan just keeps slipping further into a state of mild paralysis. The voters can't throw the rascals out because there is no one to replace them who is not already part of the problem.

Japan is nevertheless capable of reform. During the Meiji period from 1868–1912, Japan transformed itself from an isolated, decentralized, traditional society to a modern nation-state by accepting root and branch reforms at all levels of Japanese society. The Japan that emerged at the end of the American occupation in the early 1950s was likewise fundamentally different from the Japan that precipitated the Second World War in Asia in the 1930s. When the Japanese people believe that reform is necessary, they can act with astonishing speed and effectiveness. It remains to be seen how long it will take for them to awake from their slumber.

Philippines

History

When I was about six years old, we lived in the Philippines for a year where my father taught at Philippine Women's University on a Fulbright. It was just a few years after the end of the Second World War in 1945, and after the Philippines had acquired its independence from the United States in 1946 (on July 4). One of my distinct memories is the view of Manila Bay littered with the hulls of ships sunk during the war and awaiting salvage. The city itself contained blocks of bombed-out buildings in which people still lived, eking out a meager living in the ruins. Jeepneys, taxis converted from American jeeps, were the standard mode of transportation, along with crowded buses. Everywhere there was motion and everywhere there was the warmth of the Filipino personality. After we returned home my father would often recall a conversation with a colleague during that year in which his friend said something to the effect that he would rather have a Philippines run like hell by Filipinos than one run like heaven by Americans. Then he followed that up with a smile and said: 'And that's exactly what we've got!'

To understand the achievements and failures of Filipino democracy, one has to begin with geography and history. The Philippines, off the south-eastern corner of the Eurasian continent, is composed of more than 7,000 islands, the most important of which is Luzon. Peopled by waves of migration from mainland Eurasia and from the Indonesian archipelago, Filipinos are descendants primarily of Malay ancestors. Their first contact with Europeans came in 1521 when Ferdinand Magellan landed in the Philippines during his voyage around the world – and was actually killed there. (Magellan still gets credit for sailing around the world because he had previously sailed from Southeast Asia to Europe, and because some of his sailors did in fact make it back to Europe safely.) Spain used Magellan's landfall to claim sovereignty over the islands, which they named the Philippine Islands in honor of the heir to the Spanish throne, who became King Philip II. Spanish rule over the Philippines for the next three centuries firmly implanted the Spanish language as well as Roman Catholicism on Filipino culture.

After the Americans wrested the Philippines away from Spain in the Spanish-American War in 1898, the Americans took steps to build the foundations of self-rule in the Philippines. Congress passed legislation in 1902 establishing a bicameral legislature in the Philippines. When the Philippine assembly met for the first time in 1907 it became the first elective legislature in Southeast Asia. Woodrow Wilson promised full independence to the Philippines, but American politics slowed the process down until Franklin Delano Roosevelt crafted a bill in Congress granting commonwealth status to the Philippines from 1934, with the promise of full independence in twelve years. Independence, as noted above, was granted on July 4, 1946. The Philippines adopted a structure of government based on the American model, and the first presidents commanded the widespread respect of the country.

Democracy lasted until 1972, when President Ferdinand Marcos declared martial law and ruled by decree until 1981. He was finally overthrown in

1986 by a popular movement led by Corazon Aquino, the widow of Benigno Aquino, an opposition leader who had been murdered in 1983. She was elected president by an overwhelming majority of the population and was succeeded by a former general, Fidel Ramos. In 1998, Ramos was in turn succeeded by the aging actor Joseph Estrada, who won in a landslide. Although allegations of corruption resulted in his impeachment in the House of Representatives, his trial in the Senate was interrupted by widespread public demands for his replacement. In January 2001 his position was declared vacant and he was succeeded by Vice-President Gloria Macapagal Arroyo, the daughter of a previous president of the Philippines. Many commentators worried that the suspension of an orderly process of impeachment and trial boded ill for democratic processes in the Philippines.

Institutions

The institutional structure of Philippine democracy is solid on the outside. The president is elected by universal suffrage, as are senators and members of the House of Representatives. Because of the Marcos precedent, the president is now limited to one term. Elections are in general free, fair, and reasonably frequent. Freedom of expression is widespread and there are numerous avenues through which a full range of political views can be expressed: newspapers, television, radio, and, of course, the Internet. There are few limits on alternative sources of information, and there are few limits on the freedom to associate in groups. Some observers have pointed to the latter as one of the most promising developments in Philippine democracy. Non-governmental organizations have played an increasingly significant role in stimulating popular participation in the political process, particularly since Aquino's 'people power' movement that ousted the Marcos regime in the mid-1980s.[9] Citizenship is inclusive.

On the surface, therefore, Philippine democracy appears successful. It is only by looking more deeply that the serious limitations begin to appear. The first weakness is lack of access to positions of power by the vast majority of the population. Most of the power in the Philippines is concentrated in the hands of a small number of families who own the bulk of the land in the countryside and who control most of the political power and patronage in the country as a whole. This pattern of landholding is a remnant of the long period of Spanish colonization. Its consequence is to impoverish the rural population and cultivate a popular mentality of helplessness that the families then exploit to their own advantage. Given the disparity in power, the temptation to corruption is irresistible. The two decades of Marcos's dictatorship witnessed such a looting of the country's wealth by these families that the country fell into economic and political paralysis.

Hopes were high when Aquino took over in 1986, but she lacked the leadership to challenge the power of the great families, including her own.

Fidel Ramos, who succeeded her, likewise did not address this problem. His successor, in turn, the former actor Joseph Estrada, revived the corrupt practices of the past until he was ousted. Since the members of the Senate are largely drawn from the influential families, they are unlikely to support reform efforts that would undermine their own power and status. Realistic reform will probably require a long period of popular education and mobilization by organizations outside the government such as the Roman Catholic Church.

Conditions

The essential conditions for democracy in the Philippines are not all favorable. The most troubling is the interference of the military in politics. During Corazon Aquino's presidency from 1986 to 1992, there were no fewer than seven coup attempts by the military. Her successor Fidel Ramos was spared only because he himself was a former military officer who had been the key figure in putting down the coup attempts in the previous administration. The lack of professionalism in the Philippine military fostered during the Marcos period remains one of the greatest dangers to Philippine democracy.

The political culture in the Philippines, in terms of its commitment to democracy, is mixed. On the one hand there is a strong popular faith in the justice of democratic institutions that was manifested in the People's Power movement that overthrew Ferdinand Marcos. On the other hand, the Spanish legacy of local 'family power,' the stifling and corrupt bureaucracy of government, the lack of competition among industries, the inability of the ruling elite to put the public interest above their private profit, all undermine the public's confidence in democracy. At least there are no longer any foreign powers who dominate Philippine affairs. On the contrary, one wishes that the United States, when it did have such control, might have initiated the same kind of rural landholding reform in the Philippines that it did in Japan after the Second World War. Instead the United States acquiesced to the interests of the families and to the detriment of the average farmer.

Neither does the Philippines enjoy entirely favorable (as opposed to essential) conditions for a thriving democracy. To be sure, there is a market economy tied to international trade. During the 1950s and 1960s, the Philippine economy was among the most prosperous and promising in Asia. The Marcos regime, however, so plundered the assets of the country that it will take decades to recover. The climate of corruption and exploitation has been so pervasive that even fifteen years after the fall of Marcos the government has been unable to make substantial progress in reversing the crony capitalism of the Marcos years. The over-centralization of power, together with the widespread poverty in both cities and the countryside, have provided opportunities for rural insurgencies in the southern Philippines that have further undermined the credibility of the government and the military.

Those insurgencies are exacerbated by the widespread differences between linguistic and ethnic minorities in the Philippines. Only slightly more than half of the population speak Filipino (based on Tagalog), the national language. The rest speak local languages and dialects, and English. Although the vast majority of the people are Roman Catholic, about 5 percent are Muslim who live in the southern islands near Indonesia. Their persistent claims for independence, backed up by kidnapping and violence, have damaged economic development as well as faith in the effectiveness of the central government. In spite of all these challenges, however, the prognosis for democracy in the Philippines is still favorable. With time and the continued opening up of the market economy to the stimulus of global trade, the middle class will be unlikely to accept the status quo indefinitely. As they agitate for change, the precedent of the People Power movement will no doubt be a powerful inspiration.

Conclusion

The three countries of India, Japan, and the Philippines are all democracies. As such they share many qualities of government with all other democracies, such as real elections and free institutions. They also have differences. India represents a successful democracy in which a huge percentage of the electorate is illiterate. Japan presents a successful democracy in which only one party has dominated government for decades. The Philippines presents a successful democracy that has alternated with periods of authoritarian rule and in which a small elite exercise inordinate influence over public affairs.

What conclusions can we draw from these similarities and differences? First of all, democracy is never perfect. It partakes of all the temptations and shortcomings that afflict the human personality, not the least of which are egoism and greed. The struggle to put the public good above private interest is universal and it is unceasing. It remains the central challenge of every democracy, whether Asian, British, Canadian, or American. Second, democracy never takes place in a laboratory but in a specific country with institutions that derive from a unique culture and history. The freedoms that people enjoy, in other words, are all made possible by the authority of specific institutions. In the case of India and the Philippines, many of those institutions stem from their colonial heritage as well as indigenous sources. In the case of Japan, the basic institutions that constitute the larger context of authority represent a synthesis of local traditions and European and American models of governance. In all cases, the two qualities of freedom and authority are complementary but there is always a tendency for one to grow at the expense of the other. The key is balance. Too much freedom produces anarchy, and too much authority produces tyranny. In the three countries we have considered in this chapter, the task is to arrive at the proper balance in the context of each country's differing heritage.

They also face the never-ending challenge of all democracies to reach a proper balance between the often conflicting demands of freedom and equality. If, through corruption or abuse of power, the rewards of land, labor, and capital flow disproportionately to one small sector of society, those who are denied those rewards are unable to develop their own talents and place them at the service of society as a whole. Imagine, for example, how much talent is wasted in a society where the bulk of the population is so poor that it cannot afford the education necessary to bring their potential to fruition. If those inequalities become too extreme, the disenfranchised will eventually become so alienated that they will work to overthrow the system. This is the concern in India and the Philippines. If, on the other hand, the rewards of land, labor, and capital are spread so equitably to everyone in the name of group solidarity, then the freedom to create and innovate are stifled. Japan, for example, has created a system in which the pieces are so interconnected that it appears virtually impossible to initiate sweeping reforms. Any individual who tries to change one part of the system encounters such massive resistance from all the other parts that progress is virtually impossible. Here, then, in the relationship between freedom and equality as in the relationship between freedom and authority, the challenge is to find a balance.

Notes

1 Professor Steve Muhlberger has written a draft article entitled 'Democracy in India,' which is available on his website mentioned at the end of this chapter (nipissingu.ca/department/history/muhlberger/histdem). See also the master-piece on Indian culture by A.L. Basham, *The Wonder that was India* (New York: Grove Press, 1954), pp. 96–98. The quotation comes from R.C. Majumdar's *Corporate Life in Ancient India* (Calcutta: Firma K.L. Mukhopadhyay, 1969), p. 219.

2 From the *Nitisara* (The Science of Polity) by Shukracharya, quoted in Jawaharlal Nehru's *Discovery of India* (London: Meridian Books, 1956), p. 244.

3 Shalendra D. Sharma, *Development and Democracy in India* (Boulder: Lynne Rienner, 1999), p. 8.

4 *Discovery of India* (London: Meridian Books, 1956), p. 253.

5 Amartya Sen, *Development as Freedom* (New York: Alfred A. Knopf, 1999).

6 One of the most interesting interpretations of this point of view is Karel van Wolferen, *The Enigma of Japanese Power: People and Politics in a Stateless Nation* (New York: Vintage Books, 1990).

7 *Economist* (July 1, 2000), p. 28.

8 Karel van Wolferen, op. cit., p. 272. Wolferen is pessimistic about Japan's ability to reform itself because, as he puts it, 'no one is ultimately in charge' (p. 5).

9 For a fascinating discussion of this development, see G. Sidney Silliman and Lela Garner Noble, 'Citizen Movements and Philippine Democracy,' in *Organizing for Democracy: NGOs, Civil Society, and the Philippine State* (Honolulu: University of Hawai'i Press, 1998), pp. 280–310.

Further reading

India

One of the best starting points for an understanding of Indian politics is Robert L. Hardgrave, Jr, and Stanley A. Kochanek's textbook, *India: Government and Politics in a Developing Nation* (Orlando: Harcourt Brace Publishers, 2000). For an excellent scholarly account see Paul Brass's *Politics of India Since Independence* (Cambridge: Cambridge University Press, 1990). A cautiously optimistic treatment of the effect of Hindu nationalism on Indian democracy can be found in Thomas Blom Hansen, *The Saffron Wave: Democracy and Hindu Nationalism in Modern India* (Princeton: Princeton University Press, 1999). Atul Kohli draws more pessimistic conclusions in *Democracy and Discontent: India's Growing Crisis of Governability* (Cambridge: Cambridge University Press, 1990). See also his *India's Democracy: An Analysis of Changing State–Society Relations* (Princeton: Princeton University Press, 1990). Shalendra D. Sharma argues that civil society in India is losing its ability to transcend parochial and local interests in *Development and Democracy in India* (Boulder: Lynne Rienner, 1999). For coverage of the relationship between Indian democracy and rural India, see Ashutosh Varshney, *Democracy, Development, and the Countryside* (Cambridge: Cambridge University Press, 1995). To explore the contribution of democracy to economic reform, consult Rob Jenkins, *Democratic Politics and Economic Reform in India* (New York: Cambridge University Press, 1999).

Japan

For a comparative view of East Asian democracies, see Edward Friedman, ed., *The Politics of Democratization: Generalizing East Asian Experiences* (Boulder: Westview Press, 1994). Peter J. Herzog's *Japan's Pseudo-Democracy* (New York: New York University Press, 1993) focuses on the weaknesses of Japanese democracy. Takeshi Ishida and Ellis S. Krauss's edited collection of academic monographs *Democracy in Japan* (Pittsburgh: University of Pittsburgh Press, 1989) provides a useful scholarly perspective on selected topics. Krauss's *Japan's Democracy: How Much Change?* (Ithaca: Foreign Policy Association, 1995) is a very helpful overview, as is Gavan McCormack and Yoshio Sugimoto's edited collection of studies entitled *Democracy in Contemporary Japan* (New York: M.E. Sharpe, 1986). For a scholarly treatment that argues persuasively for the vitality of Japanese democracy see Bradley Richardson, *Japanese Democracy: Power, Coordination, and Performance* (New Haven: Yale University Press, 1997). See also Gerald Leon Curtis, *The Japanese Way of Politics* (New York: Columbia University Press, 1988); Ronald Hrebenar, *The Japanese Party System* (Boulder: Westview Press, 1992); and Susan Pharr, *Losing Face: Status Politics in Japan* (Berkeley: University of California Press, 1990). A journalistic treatment can be found in Frank McNeil, *Democracy in Japan: The Emerging Global Concern* (New York: Crown Publishers, 1994).

Philippines

Two useful collections of academic monographs on selected topics of Philippine democracy are G. Sidney Silliman and Lela G. Noble's *Organizing for Democracy: NGOs, Civil Society, and the Philippine State* (Honolulu: University of Hawai'i Press,

1998), and Felipe B. Miranda, *Democratization: Philippine Perspectives* (Honolulu: University of Hawai'i Press, 1999). For a treatment of the undemocratic legacy of authoritarian rule in the Philippines, see Gretchen Casper, *Fragile Democracies: The Legacies of Authoritarian Rule* (Pittsburgh: University of Pittsburgh Press, 1995). Jeffrey M. Riedinger's *Agrarian Reform in the Philippines: Democratic Transitions and Redistributive Reform* (Stanford: Stanford University Press, 1995) offers a sobering account of the obstacles to genuine agrarian reform in the Philippines. A section on Philippine democracy and development is contained in Thomas Robinson's edited book entitled *Democracy and Development in East Asia: Taiwan, South Korea, and the Philippines* (Washington, DC: The AEI Press, 1991). For additional coverage of Philippine politics, see Jennifer Conroy Franco, *Elections and Democratization in the Philippines* (New York: Routledge, 2001); Benedict Kerkvliet, *Everyday Politics in the Philippines* (Berkeley: University of California Press, 1990); Richard J. Kessler, *Rebellion and Repression in the Philippines* (New Haven: Yale University Press, 1989); and David Joel Steinberg, *The Philippines: A Singular and Plural Place* (Boulder: Westview Press, 1990).

Chapter 4

Later democracies in East Asia

South Korea, Taiwan, and the
prospects for China

The democracies that developed in South Korea and Taiwan are different from the post-war democracies of Japan, the Philippines, and India, where the institutions of democracy were built upon pre-war foundations (in the case of Japan), or they were continuations of a colonial legacy left behind by the United States (in the case of the Philippines) and Great Britain (in the case of India) at independence. Democracies in South Korea and Taiwan, on the other hand, both developed out of an authoritarian political tradition, once again illustrating a basic theme of this work, namely that there can be multiple paths to a fully democratic polity. Their experience is significant for another reason as well. Both societies are profoundly influenced (as was Japan) by the Confucian ethic.

Oddly enough, for most of the twentieth century, intellectuals throughout East Asia blamed the Confucian heritage for the relative weakness of China and Korea in the face of European imperialism. It was thought that the Confucian respect for family, for the past, and for authority, prevented the rapid economic and technological progress characteristic of the West. By the end of the twentieth century, however, the miraculous economic growth in Japan, South Korea, Hong Kong, Singapore, Taiwan, and China has led many intellectuals to reassess that tradition. Although there were undoubtedly aspects of the Confucian heritage that might be considered harmful to rapid economic growth, there also appeared to be other characteristics – such as respect for education, discipline, hard work, and cooperation – that were beneficial.

Samuel P. Huntington, in his influential study on democracy, posits a fundamental incompatibility between the Confucian heritage and modern democratic practice. At the same time, he does acknowledge that for the same reason the Confucian heritage was once thought to have hindered economic progress and now appears to have promoted it, the Confucian heritage may also have 'some elements that are compatible with democracy.'[1] He further notes, quite correctly, that cultures are dynamic entities, always changing in response to new challenges. Confucianism in fact went through a major adaptation during the Song dynasty, during which it responded to spiritual challenges posed by an Indian import to China – Buddhism. The result was a neo-Confucian synthesis that became the dominant form of Confucianism to the present day not only in China but also in Korea and Japan. Once Chinese intellectuals are freed from the political control of the Communist Party, they may well begin another process of synthesizing the Chinese heritage with the ideas now pouring in from the West.

Meanwhile, the transition of Taiwan to a full democracy is especially significant because it is the first time in Chinese history that the threshold from authoritarian to democratic rule has been crossed. What we can now hope for is that Taiwan and other overseas Chinese can play the same mentoring role in politics that they have played in economics by helping China make the transition from a command to a market economy. Since the Chinese people constitute almost one-quarter of the human race, and since the Chinese economy will quite likely become the largest economy in the world within another generation, it is vitally important for the future peace of the world that China make a smooth transition from the totalitarian rule of the Communist Party to a full democracy as soon as possible. For this reason I have included a discussion on China even though it is not yet democratic. In South Korea and Taiwan we are talking about reality. In China we are talking about the future.

South Korea

History

Koreans often refer to their country as a shrimp caught between two whales: Japan and China. The fact is that although Korea is indeed sandwiched between these two much larger countries, and although both of them have invaded and occupied Korea at different points over the centuries, the Koreans have developed a distinctive culture of their own. The first Korean dynasty for which we have historic records dates back to the first century BC when it was conquered by Han dynasty China. Contact with China over the centuries led to the Koreans adopting three main influences from China: its written language, Buddhism, and Confucianism. In all cases, however, the Koreans shaped those influences to conform to their own cultural values and traditions.

The Korean language is fundamentally different from the Chinese language and is thought to have descended (along with Japanese) from the Altaic languages spoken in Central Asia. Although the Chinese script was used by educated Koreans until the fairly recent past, a fully alphabetic script was developed by the brilliant Korean King Sejon and promulgated in 1446. This script is the one used by Koreans today. In a similar manner, Korean Buddhism developed its own schools and doctrines, some of which in turn influenced the development of Buddhist scholarship in Japan and China as well. Confucianism in Korea was also adapted to the particular circumstances of Korean social life, which was dominated by a powerful hereditary aristocracy. (In China the aristocracy had disappeared after the fall of the Tang dynasty in 906.)

From 918 to 1392 Korea was unified under the Koryo dynasty, from which the modern English name of the country derives. During its almost 500-year run, the dynasty achieved a high standard of cultural and political achievement, but also suffered from an invasion by the Mongols in the thirteenth century. In 1392 a new dynasty was founded – the Chosun or Yi dynasty – that lasted until 1910. Strongly influenced by the Chinese doctrine of neo-Confucianism, the Chosun dynasty enjoyed a long period of political stability. The governing elite, albeit drawn from the aristocracy, were chosen mostly by examination, insuring for the most part a high level of public service. In 1592 Korea's vulnerability to threats from the outside world was reinforced by an invasion from Japan. The Japanese were soon expelled with the help of Chinese armies sent by the Ming emperor.

By the end of the nineteenth century, Korea had opened up to the outside world but experienced a gradual increase in Japanese influence. After 1895, when Japan defeated China in the Sino-Japanese war, Japanese control over Korean affairs increased dramatically. In 1910 Korea was formally annexed by Japan. For the next thirty-five years, Koreans lost their sovereignty altogether. They were forced to study Japanese in the school system, were compelled to orient their industry to serve Japan, and many hundreds of thousands were forcibly relocated to Japan to provide labor for Japanese industry. Eventually even the Korean language was outlawed by the Japanese occupiers. The legacy of this period has been a deep-seated animosity by the Koreans against the Japanese, which has only slightly abated in the last half-century. The most recent expression of this underlying resentment occurred when dozens of elderly Korean women stepped forward in the 1990s to demand an apology from Japan for having been forced to serve Japanese soldiers as prostitutes during the Second World War. The persistent refusal by the Japanese government to acknowledge the past injuries inflicted by the Japanese military insures that these old wounds will continue to fester.

After the defeat of Japan in the Second World War, Korea was occupied in the area north of the 38th parallel by the Soviet Union, who installed Kim Il Sung as leader, and south of the parallel by the United States, who installed Syngman Rhee as ruler. By 1948 it was clear that unification could not be achieved, and the Republic of South Korea (ROK) and the Democratic People's Republic of Korea (DPRK) were established. Within two years they were at war with each other. The conflict lasted from 1950 to 1953, brought about the massive intervention of Chinese troops, and accomplished nothing. The result was a stalemate, with the same people in power controlling the same territory that they had before the war began. One of the most destructive wars of modern times, the Korean War is estimated to have killed almost 2 million Koreans, up to two-thirds of whom were civilians. The

Chinese lost almost a million troops. The American death toll was about 54,000, with more than 100,000 wounded.

In 1960, Rhee was forced to step down as president after popular demonstrations protested his blatant manipulation of the previous election. His successor lasted only a few months before the military staged a coup in 1961 under the leadership of Park Chung Hee, who ruled essentially as a dictator until 1979 when he was assassinated. Park presided over a period of political repression but remarkable economic growth, both of which continued under his successor General Chun Doo Hwan. Mass protest demonstrations against his rule occurred in the 1980s, and in 1987 he agreed to a series of democratic reforms that included the adoption of a new constitution and the election of his close associate General Roh Tae Woo as president in the same year.

In 1990 Roh formed the Democratic Liberal Party by joining with former dissident Kim Young Sam. Forced to resign amid allegations of electoral irregularities in 1992, Roh was succeeded as president by Kim in national democratic elections. During Kim's administration the economy ran into serious difficulties. Kim's leadership was compromised by a series of corruption scandals among top leaders in the government. In 1997 the opposition leader Kim Dae Jung (no relation to Kim Young Sam), who had spent his public career as a champion of democracy, often in prison, was elected president. This election was particularly significant because it was the first time in Korean history that the electorate had turned out the ruling party and replaced it with the leader of an opposition party. The equivalent milestone occurred in Taiwan in the year 2000, as we shall see below, when the opposition leader Chen Shui-bian was elected president of the Republic of China. Toward the end of his term in office, Kim Dae Jung was also plagued by allegations of scandal directed against members of his own family. By the end of 2002, relations with North Korea appeared to be warming (in spite of North Korea having announced it possessed nuclear weapons), and there was talk of restoring communication and transportation links between the North and the South. In December 2002, Roh Moo Hyun, a former human rights lawyer, and the candidate of Kim's Millennium Democratic Party, was elected president on a platform of continuing to maintain dialogue with the North.

Institutions

The institutional structure of democracy in South Korea is healthy. Dating from the late 1980s, the principal leaders of the central government have been elected in an electoral process that is free, fair, and frequent. Freedom of the press is now an accepted fixture on the political landscape. The population is routinely presented with a variety of different perspectives in both the print and broadcast media, and access to the Internet is growing rapidly and further broadening the points of view accessible to the voting public. Groups have the freedom to associate without interference on the part of the government. University students have been a significant catalyst for change in Korea over the years. Indeed, it was largely because of demonstrations by students that democracy was finally achieved in Korea in the late 1980s. Citizenship is inclusive.

Democracy in South Korea is far from perfect, however. There are two fundamental weaknesses: personalism and factionalism. These two weaknesses in the institutional makeup of Korean democracy will be difficult to remedy. Political parties tend to base their membership on personal loyalty rather than a commitment to policies or principles. This reinforces a centralizing impulse and makes policy the result of the whim of the leader rather than a result of more predictable principles. The second is a tendency to break down political associations on the basis of regional loyalties. Each of the last two leaders has his strongest base of support in a particular region of Korea, which dilutes his credibility as a spokesman for the country as a whole.

Both of these weaknesses, as well as the strengths of Korean democracy, were on display during the presidency of Kim Dae Jung. First the strengths: by all accounts he was more successful than his predecessor Kim Young Sam in implementing both economic reform and democratic consolidation. In the former arena he secured the cooperation rather than the animosity of the Korean labor movement in his efforts to jettison inefficient companies, he weeded out insolvent banks and credit institutions, and encouraged over-centralized conglomerates (known as *chaebol*) to restructure. To accomplish this goal he actively cultivated public support in the population at large. To be successful, however, he had to rely for support on more traditional, and less democratic, institutions. He filled important posts with representatives from his own region. He relied on government initiatives to the exclusion of legislative involvement, preferring speed and efficiency in implementing reforms rather than the more cumbersome process of building coalition support in the National Assembly.

There are some who argue that the pain required in order to implement reforms in the economy, such as massive unemployment resulting from allowing inefficient industries to go bankrupt, is so great that democratic government cannot survive in Korea. Only an authoritarian government has the capacity to endure short-term pain for long-term gain. Those who take this position often cite the Philippines as an example of a government seemingly so paralyzed by the magnitude of the task it faces that it is unable to act. However much that may be the case in the Philippines, the administration of Kim Dae Jung in South Korea may be evidence for the counter-proposition, that it is possible to undertake painful reform while simultaneously building the foundation of a successful democracy. The final outcome, of course, will be revealed only in the future.

Conditions

In terms of the essential conditions for Korean democracy, the prospects are mixed but improving. In the past the military has repeatedly usurped power and stifled democracy. It is important, however, to put this issue in the larger context of the legacy of the Korean War and the reality of a divided Korea. The military threat from North Korea is real and of long standing. Under such circumstances it is perhaps understandable that the military would play a stronger role in government than during periods of peace and security. There is some truth to the military's claim that during periods of national emergency their role ought to be enhanced. And enhance they did. General Park Chung Hee usurped power in 1961, as did General Chun Doo Hwan in 1980. Chun's successor as president, Roh Tae Woo, was also a general in the army. Since the early 1990s, however, the army has not openly intervened in politics. One of Kim Young Sam's major accomplishments in his term of office was to dismantle the association of military officers that had provided them with a political base.

There is no question of the Korean people's commitment to democracy, especially as the population continues to become more educated and more urban. Knowledgeable observers, however, caution that the institutional roots of democracy remain relatively shallow. Local government is only a recent development, all local issues previously having been decided by agencies of the central government. Heavily influenced by the Confucian heritage, Korean society is hierarchical and paternalistic with a strong belief in the responsibility of government to act as a parent overseeing the welfare of its people. A large percentage of the population look back with nostalgia at the days of Park Chung Hee, when there was less corruption and more 'harmony' in the body politic.

Nevertheless, the grounds for optimism are enhanced by the simple fact that South Korea is no longer subject, as it was for so many years under Japanese rule, to a country hostile to democracy. In addition, its commitment to a market economy and to a pluralistic society is strong and likely to become even stronger. There are no ethnic minorities of any significance to act as an obstacle to building a political consensus, though regional loyalties remain strong and often interfere with those who want to build a system of national parties. On balance, the successes of Korean democracy are remarkable, and justify an optimistic assessment of continued maturity in the future.

Taiwan

History

Four hundred years ago, Taiwan was a small and beautiful island 300 miles off the eastern coast of China inhabited primarily by indigenous tribal peoples speaking an Austronesian language. From the beginning of the Qing dynasty in China in 1644, increasing numbers of ethnic Chinese from the coastal province of Fujian migrated to Taiwan, gradually driving the indigenous people into the mountains. By the end of the nineteenth century, Taiwan had become fully incorporated into the Chinese state. In 1895, however, as a result of China's loss to Japan in the Sino-Japanese War, Taiwan was ceded to Japan and occupied by Japanese troops. For the next fifty years, until the end of the Second World War in 1945, the Japanese tried to impose their culture on Taiwan, forcing the Chinese to attend school in Japanese and denying them access to higher education except in the field of medicine.

After the defeat of Japan, Taiwan reverted to Chinese suzerainty and was occupied by Nationalist troops of the Republic of China, who were themselves engaged in a civil war on mainland China with Communist forces led by Mao Zedong. Initially welcomed on Taiwan as liberators from Japanese rule, the Nationalists managed through corrupt and incompetent leadership to provoke an uprising in February 1947 that was ruthlessly suppressed. In 1949 the Republic of China on the mainland was defeated by Communist troops and retreated to the island of Taiwan, where, led by Chiang Kai-shek, it set up a government in exile claiming to be the legitimate ruler of all of China. The People's Republic of China, meanwhile, continued to occupy the Chinese mainland and also claimed to be the legitimate ruler of all of China. The stalemate between the two governments, each claiming authority over the other, has remained in place for the last half-century.

The government in Taiwan, while led by the Kuomintang Party (KMT) under the leadership of Chiang Kai-shek until his death in 1975, could best be described as authoritarian. Chiang repressed political opposition and imposed martial law that lasted until after his death. Although he was repeatedly elected president, the National Assembly that elected him was composed of members who had themselves been elected in mainland China in 1948. As time passed they became increasingly aged but were not replaced. Chiang's KMT instituted a sweeping reform of land tenure in Taiwan, granting full ownership to tenant farmers and transforming the countryside. The reform was so successful that many observers speculated that he never would have lost the civil war to Mao Zedong if he had implemented these reform measures in China itself. Responding to those criticisms, the KMT noted, with much truth, that it was impossible to implement that kind of reform in China while fighting a debilitating war with the Japanese. In any case, Chiang also presided over what can only be described as spectacular economic growth in the 1950s and 1960s, producing increases in GDP that were the envy of the world. He may not have been committed to democratic principles, but in the realm of economic development he opened Taiwan up to the world market and engineered one of the most successful periods of economic growth in modern times.

When Chiang died in 1975, his son Chiang Ching-kuo succeeded him as leader of the KMT and continued the policies of economic growth that had been initiated by his father. Having spent years in the Soviet Union as a young man, Chiang's ascension to power did not inspire confidence among those hoping for democratic reforms. But Chiang Ching-kuo surprised his critics, and represents a remarkable example of how important effective leadership can be to the success of democratic institutions. He set about promoting native Taiwanese (descendants of Chinese who had migrated into the area during the Qing dynasty, as opposed to the mainland Chinese who arrived in the late 1940s) and reforming the electoral system. Over time he changed the makeup of the KMT from a party whose leadership was composed entirely of mainland Chinese to one that accurately reflected the demographic reality of Taiwan itself: about 85 percent composed of native Taiwanese. By the mid-1980s his diabetes had reached the point where he knew he had very little time left. Determined to lay the institutional foundations for democracy in Taiwan, he legalized political opposition to the KMT and in 1987 abolished martial law. He died in 1988.

He was succeeded as president by Lee Teng-hui, a native Taiwanese with an American Ph.D. in agricultural economics from Cornell University. Lee continued the process of opening up the political life of Taiwan, presiding over the transition to full and complete freedom of the press. As leader of the KMT, he won reelection to the presidency in 1990 and again in 1996, the second time in a new electoral system based on direct popular election of the president. To him, as well as to Chiang Ching-kuo, goes much of the credit for overseeing the peaceful transition to a fully democratic system. By skillful maneuvering he managed to reconcile the social and political divisions of the country sufficiently to retain public confidence in the processes of government. In May 2000, for the first time in Chinese history, the final hurdle of a maturing democracy was overcome when the sitting government dominated by the KMT was turned out of office and replaced by a leader of the opposition party. Chen Shui-bian, another native-born Taiwanese who had served as Mayor of Taipei as well as head of the Democratic Progressive Party (DPP), was elected president. In so doing, Taiwan crossed the same institutional threshold that South Korea had in 1998 when the leader of the opposition party, Kim Dae Jung, was elected president there.

Institutions

As mentioned above, the entire electoral system in Taiwan was reformed in the 1990s, first to elect members of the national legislature directly on the basis of universal suffrage, then to elect the president directly. Elections have been free, fair, and frequent. The print media are now completely free to express themselves without interference from the state, and there are a multitude of sources of information on all political positions. The one remaining anomaly of the media is the ownership by the Kuomintang Party of the three main television stations in Taiwan, granting the KMT leverage over the content that is not in accord with democratic principles. The vast business interests in which the KMT has invested also give the party access to funds not available to other parties, and emphasizes the importance of money in politics in a way that is corrupting and unhealthy (as Americans can attest as well!). That is likely to change now that they have lost control of the government. There are limited restrictions on association of civic groups, and citizenship is inclusive. There are, in short, few if any institutional barriers to complete democracy in Taiwan today. The essential challenges lie in the realm of conditions.

Conditions

The essential conditions for democracy in Taiwan are all present, though to what degree is a matter of interpretation. The military and police are for the most part under the effective control of elected officials. The principle of civilian authority was established during the period of Chiang Ching-kuo's rule. His father, Chiang Kai-shek, had been a general himself before assuming what was essentially a civilian role after moving his government to Taiwan in the late 1940s. The only area of concern is the extensive involvement of the military in ownership of real estate, industrial interests, and even trade. One would hope that with time these involvements in areas outside the formal responsibilities of the military for defense can be significantly reduced.

The deeper question of to what degree there exist democratic beliefs and a political culture supporting democracy is more complex. There is no doubt that public support for democratic institutions is wide and deep. Many observers have remarked, however, on the immaturity of behavior and attitude expressed by many legislators in Taiwan as they adapt to new responsibilities. Members of the KMT, who found themselves out of power for the first time after the election of Chen Shui-bian as president in 2000, control the legislature and have had difficulty putting the interests of the country ahead of their desire to regain power, and setting aside personal animosities in order to work together. This phenomenon is, of course, not unknown in other democracies, but there is a point at which politicians have to set aside their differences and consider the welfare of the country as a whole. That point has sometimes been difficult to find for many politicians in Taiwan. In terms of the rule of law, Taiwan has fully matured, and experiences no greater degree of failure than any other institution administered by fallible human beings.

At the moment, there is no strong foreign control hostile to democracy, but the relationship between Taiwan and mainland China is so complex and unpredictable that it looms over all discussions of the future. China is willing to allow the status quo to continue only as long as Taiwan does not declare its 'independence,' that is, repudiate the assertion held for decades by the KMT that Taiwan is a part of China. The DPP, although it advocated independence during the years when it was in opposition, has modified its position after it won the presidency and expressed a willingness to discuss the issue with the mainland government. China, for its part, has made alarming noises about using force to recover Taiwan at some unspecified point in the future. The issue will likely remain a flash point for the foreseeable future and a potential danger to the stability of democracy on Taiwan.

The strong market-oriented economy in Taiwan is one of its most positive features in terms of fostering the conditions for a successful democracy. Indeed, those who advocate the theory that capitalism is conducive to democracy often use Taiwan as one of their strongest points of evidence. The miraculous growth in the post-war economy created a middle class that traveled broadly and brought to bear on the government increasing pressure to open up politics as effectively as it had opened up the economy. This experience is also one of the strongest indications that Taiwan may serve as a model for democracy in China. Not only is there an ethnic tie between the two countries, but there is also the experience of moving from an authoritarian system (both the KMT and the Chinese Communist Party – the CCP – were originally organized by representatives of the Soviet Comintern in the 1920s) that opened up the country to a market and trade-oriented capitalist economy.

The last shadow cast across an otherwise shining example of the transition to democracy in Taiwan has to do with the potential for ethnic conflict to erode a common sense of national identity. Approximately 10–15 percent of the population in Taiwan are mainland Chinese – or descendents of mainland Chinese – who came to Taiwan in the late 1940s. For decades they dominated the government in Taiwan (though native Taiwanese dominated the economic sector). During their rule the Taiwanese language – actually a Min dialect from Fujian – was not allowed to be used on television or radio, and expressions of indigenous Taiwanese culture were discouraged. In addition, the memory of the brutality of the repression in February 28, 1947 festered beneath the surface for many Taiwanese. When the Nationalists were voted out of office in 2000, these long-repressed emotions bubbled to the surface and lie behind many of the conflicts that have arisen in the past few years. Although there is considerable evidence that these issues are receding in importance as Taiwan faces the larger issue of what to do about China, they nevertheless form the background to any understanding of politics in Taiwan, and will influence the evolution of political institutions there for some time to come.

China

Paradoxically, there is far more scholarly output on democracy in mainland China, where democracy doesn't exist, than there is on Taiwan, where democracy does exist. Part of the reason, no doubt, is wishful thinking. The greater part is probably due to the disparity in size and world significance. China represents almost a quarter of the human population on earth. The reality is that the future stability of world politics may well depend on whether China can make a peaceful transition from a totalitarian to a democratic form of government. Given that in the last twenty-five years China has managed to make a remarkable transition from a communist planned economy to a quasi-capitalist market economy, the likelihood that it might be able to accomplish the same degree of change in the political realm which it accomplished in the economic realm does not seem nearly as far-fetched as it once did. Indeed, one of the most important goals of the major world powers ought to be to bring China peacefully into the family of democratic nations. In doing so it is imperative that we understand the balance of forces in China that are likely both to foster and to inhibit the development of democratic institutions.

Until now, this study of Asian democracy has confined itself only to those countries that have already crossed the institutional divide from authoritarian systems of politics to one form of democracy or another. The case for discussing China, apart from the reasons mentioned above, is also due to the strong possibility that Taiwan will serve as a model for the democratization of China itself. There are, of course, many differences. China is huge, Taiwan is small. China is totalitarian, Taiwan was authoritarian, which meant that in China the long arm of government control was vastly greater than in Taiwan for decades, snuffing out alternative forms of public discourse and inhibiting the rise of pluralistic institutions. Nevertheless, the fact that Taiwan and China share the same cultural heritage, and that China still considers Taiwan part of China, may have hitherto unexpected influence on the future of Chinese politics.

History

For the last two thousand years, China has been a unified state. For most of that time, it has been incomparably the most advanced civilization in human history in terms of many of the major indices by which that vague term 'civilization' is measured: economic prosperity, technological development, political stability, social welfare, sophisticated intellectual and artistic achievements. Throughout this period, the ideological glue that held the country together was Confucianism, an ethical system originating with the scholar Confucius who lived approximately 551–479 BC. The doctrine that came to bear his name stressed as its core principle the concept of *ren*, or reciprocity. All things in the natural and human order were governed according to moral principles that were universal. Since everything was connected to everything else (it was assumed), a moral disturbance in the human order would trigger an equivalent disturbance in the natural order. An unworthy ruler, therefore, could expect to suffer the displeasure of heaven and have his mandate to rule revoked.

Among the most basic assumptions of Confucianism is the proposition that government exists to serve the people (rather than the other way around). One of the most prominent early Chinese political thinkers, Xunzi (Hsün-tzu), argued that government is instituted to benefit the people, and that the welfare of the population as a whole is the principal criterion by which a ruler ought to be judged. To illustrate this principle he used a navigational metaphor, writing that the people are the sea, and the ruler is a boat. The sea can support the boat, or the sea can capsize the boat. Although this was not intended to be an invitation to rebel, it does make clear where Xunzi believed the ultimate power of government to reside. The philosopher Mencius, widely regarded as second only to Confucius in influence on later Chinese political thought, wrote that 'the people are of supreme importance; the altars to the gods of Earth and grain come next; last comes the ruler.'[2] Rulers in Chinese history, understandably, did not appreciate that passage. They didn't like this one either:

> If a prince treats his subjects as his hands and feet, they will treat him as their belly and heart. If he treats them as his horses and hounds, they will treat him as a mere fellow-countryman. If he treats them as mud and weeds, they will treat him as an enemy.[3]

As the dynasties came and went over the centuries, the Chinese developed a sophisticated central bureaucracy staffed by members of an intellectual elite chosen through a system of rigorous examinations. Whereas the ruling bureaucracy in Europe was staffed mostly by those who owed their position to the accident of birth (via the aristocracy), in China the ruling elite was based upon merit. The hand of the state, moreover, was relatively light, as the country was huge and the central bureaucracy tiny, never more than about 25,000 for a population that hovered around 60 million for the first millennium and then began to rise during the Song dynasty a thousand years ago to reach 450 million by the middle of the nineteenth century. For our purposes that statistic is significant, since it meant that there was a considerable degree of local autonomy in China. The farther down the ladder the more likelihood there was of consultation among the leaders of various clans, families, guilds, and other organizations that together made decisions and solved disputes on the local level.

Unfortunately for China, the spirit of intellectual and technological innovation began to recede at precisely the same moment that it began to accelerate in Europe. By the sixteenth century China had retreated behind a newly built Great Wall, and although a new dynasty – the Qing (pronounced 'Ching') – was established in 1644, it was intensely conservative both intellectually and institutionally. Nevertheless, China was on a par with Europe in many categories of economic prosperity (such as per capita production and consumption) and probably ahead in others (such as provisions for social welfare) until the beginning of the nineteenth century. The turning point came with the Industrial Revolution, which transformed the productive capacity of Europe in the nineteenth century. From then on, the balance of power in the world shifted dramatically to favor those Europeans who now had the benefit of new technology in weapons and transportation with which to impose their will on the rest of the world. When steam power was applied to navigation by the middle of the century, Europeans had the technical means to project their power throughout the world. The golden age of colonialism that ensued in the second half of the nineteenth century left China still in formal possession of its sovereignty but subject to Western power in the form of humiliating treaties that deprived China of control over tariffs and the major seaports along the coast. In 1911 the dynasty was overthrown and a republic declared that soon dissolved into civil war.

On May 4, 1919, students from several Beijing universities marched to Tiananmen Square to protest the secret arrangements of the Versailles Peace Treaty ending the First World War that were unfavorable to China. In so doing they set off a broader movement for science and democracy that became known as the May Fourth Movement and is now regarded as the beginning of modern Chinese nationalism. Although the movement spawned many of the leaders of twentieth-century China, the ideals of the intellectuals could not be realized in the absence of the conditions and institutions that we have identified thus far as prerequisites for a successful democracy. China had to endure decades of intermittent civil war and then of invasion by the Japanese in the 1930s. During these years of turmoil the Chinese Communist Party, under Mao Zedong, gradually consolidated its hold in rural China. When the Second World War ended in 1945, Mao engaged in a four-year civil war with Chiang Kai-shek's Nationalist government, which was defeated in 1949 and fled to Taiwan (as we have noted above).

From 1949 until Mao's death in 1976, China was subjected to the harsh rule of a totalitarian state that claimed dominion over every aspect of people's lives. In the 1950s private land was confiscated in the countryside and people were herded into vast communes whose agricultural output fell so drastically that from 1959 to 1961 China suffered the greatest famine in human history. Approximately 30 million people died while the government continued to export grain to earn foreign exchange. No sooner had they recovered from this catastrophe than Mao plunged the nation into the disaster known as the Cultural Revolution. Lasting for ten years, from 1966 to 1976, this campaign was a result of Mao's desire to rid the Communist Party of his enemies and rekindle the revolutionary spirit that he believed had animated the Chinese people during his struggle to gain power. In the most active phase of the Cultural Revolution from 1966 to 1969, China almost descended into anarchy, and only after Mao's death in 1976 was it able to begin recovering from the disruption. The death toll may never be known, but the lives that were shattered and ruined during that decade numbered in the millions.

In 1978 Deng Xiaoping took over as the paramount leader in China, ushering in a period of extraordinary economic growth that has astonished the world and continues to the present. Deng was the last leader in China from the generation of Communist revolutionaries who had participated in the early struggles. He in effect dismantled the entire superstructure of the planned economy that had been constructed in the thirty years from 1949 to 1979. His policy, in support of what he called the 'Four Modernizations,' targeted agriculture, industry, the military, and technology.

At the same time that he moved China toward a capitalist, market-oriented economy, however, he remained determined to retain all political power in the hands of the Communist Party. He believed democracy to be mob rule, and having seen how destructive mobs could be during the Cultural Revolution, he was determined to avoid the chaos that he believed would follow if the Party were to relinquish power. Indeed, surveying the chaos that Russia fell into during the 1990s after the collapse of communism there, Deng was only confirmed in his prejudices. Meanwhile, the degrading effect of total power continued to gnaw away on the Communist Party, so that by the 1980s and 1990s corruption had become one of the most serious and intractable problems faced by the government.

At the same time, a democracy movement arose in China almost immediately after Mao's death and Deng's ascension to power. In 1978, anonymous posters calling for greater freedoms in politics began to appear on a wall in the outskirts of Beijing. Stunning the nation in their boldness and brilliance, the posters called for sweeping reforms in Chinese government. The most brilliant of the writers was a 28-year-old electrician by the name of Wei Jingsheng, who called for a 'Fifth Modernization' – democracy – in a poster put up on the wall in January 1978. After a few months of remarkable freedom of expression, the wall was shut down by the police. Wei Jingsheng was arrested and sentenced in 1979 to fifteen years in prison for sedition. Released in 1993, he remained uncowed and was promptly arrested again and imprisoned, followed in 1997 by his release and expulsion from China (to the United States) after having served a total of eighteen years in prison merely for advocating democracy and human rights.

The crackdown in the late 1970s was followed by the gradual relaxation of government control during the 1980s, culminating in the late 1980s in a most remarkable episode. On May 4, 1989, students from various Beijing universities marched to Tiananmen Square in conscious emulation of their predecessors seventy years earlier, demanding freedom and democracy. When called upon to leave by the authorities, they refused, and began a peaceful protest that was finally ended on the evening of June 3 and morning of June 4 by government troops. Hundreds of people were killed, thousands were wounded, and the streets of Beijing were covered with the blood of Chinese citizens who asked only for the freedom to speak and to elect their own government. The repression continued thereafter all through the 1990s and into the new century, even after the death of Deng Xiaoping in 1997. Government officials grew so paranoid about political opposition that they even persecuted an essentially harmless organization of people devoted to a form of exercise known as Falun Gong for little more than refusing to submit to governmental control.

Institutions

Needless to say, the basic institutions of democratic governance are only gradually coming into existence in China. Top national officials are typically not elected, and if they are it is by elections that offer only one viable candidate. Elections are therefore not free, fair, or frequent. Nevertheless, there are changes beginning to take place on both the national and local level. Some competition is appearing in elections, and the National People's Congress is slowly moving toward a more autonomous and professional organization that is increasingly inclined to question policies adopted by the government. On the local level, the situation is changing even more rapidly. As of the late 1980s, the government has called for village leaders to be elected for three-year terms. To be sure, there are more than a million villages in China, and the new procedures are implemented in only about a third of them. The degree of success, and the degree of autonomy that these elected officials have secured from control by local Communist Party officials vary significantly from region to region, but observers point to strong backing by the central government. Beijing leaders are trying to find some mechanism to reign in corruption, provide an outlet for peasant unrest, and encourage greater efficiency and legitimacy at the local level. The degree of ultimate success will depend on many factors as yet unknown, including the continued support of the national leadership. Pessimists point to the slow rate of change, optimists to the remarkable success of these new elections in many villages.

There is no freedom of expression in any of the media to criticize government officials. Alternative sources of information are repressed whenever possible. The government is even suspicious of the Internet, and routinely tries to exert control over computerized access to information outside governmental control. The results, as one might imagine, are mixed. The Internet remains a fascinating new ingredient in Chinese politics. No one knows what the impact will be. There is very little freedom for people to associate in political groups of any kind outside the direct control of the Communist Party. Even the slightest hint of political activity may result in a prison sentence. The court system is not independent of government control – the Party routinely manipulates the verdict to suit its own purposes. Nevertheless, there is progress in this realm, in part because of pressure exerted by foreign companies demanding a legal system that is fair and predictable, but it is slow.

On the positive side, citizenship is inclusive. Chinese do not exclude national minorities from full participation in the public sphere, as long as that participation remains subservient to the Party. And the overall inefficiency and ineffectiveness of government bureaucrats leaves many opportunities for people to associate outside of government control.

Conditions

The essential conditions for democracy in China are not much better than the institutions. Although the military and the police have traditionally been under the control of the Communist Party, the power of the military has increased after the death of Deng Xiaoping simply because his successor, Jiang Zemin, has been a weaker leader. The role of the military in putting down the Tiananmen Square demonstrations was clearly visible to the world, and the generals have not grown more sympathetic to democracy in the ensuing years. Democratic beliefs and political culture are absent from post-1949 China.

Traditional Chinese culture, on the other hand, rooted in Confucian, Daoist, and Buddhist views of moral self-cultivation within a universal moral order, always stressed the welfare of the people as the final measure of legitimacy for any given ruler (as noted above). To be sure, that was not the same as self-government or a rule of law, but it did promote the idea that rulers were subordinate, if not to the law, then to a higher moral order that governed both the human and the cosmic orders. That belief could well become the basis of a doctrine of human rights that owes at least as much to the Chinese tradition as it does to the Western tradition.

Let me mention two conditions of the Chinese past and present that are clearly favorable to the development of democratic institutions in China in the long run. First, the government has presided over a successful transition from a command economy to a market economy. One can only hope that as the middle class grows in number and influence, they will demand a greater say in the realm of government. Second, for the most part, China is culturally homogeneous. Although it does have minority cultures that resist integration into Chinese culture – such as the Tibetans and the Uighurs – they are located on the periphery of the Chinese state and would not represent a threat to the viability of democracy even if they were to break away and form more autonomous units.

Perhaps the greatest advantage China has in terms of moving toward democracy is the model of Taiwan. The irony of the present situation is considerable: the Nationalists, having lost the military confrontation with the Communists in the 1940s, have, in an odd sort of way, won. Their economic system and now their political system have succeeded, while the economic and political systems established by the Communists in China have failed. Now it is the Communists who, corrupt and incompetent, have lost the mandate of the people, and the Nationalists who won the mandate (even at the expense of losing power). When I last visited Shanghai, for example, I heard that there were approximately 300,000 to 500,000 businessmen from Taiwan living and doing business in the city. In effect, Taiwan has successfully invaded China without ever firing a shot.

Conclusion

One of the scholarly debates among observers of the democratic experience is over the relative significance of economic, social, cultural, political, and personal causes. These debates are important not only because they bring us closer to a true and accurate understanding of the past but also because they enable us to formulate more effective policies in the present and future. Although this study is not the place to take sides in those debates, or to declare one interpretation the winner, it is worth noting the various positions so that the reader can apply them to the great public issues of our own day.

East Asia is a case study of the close connection between a productive economic system and a successful democracy. The principle goes something like this: economic growth over time promotes the rise of an educated middle class with an interest in political stability. As this middle class grows in sophistication and exposure to the outside world, it develops a greater sense of its own political power and a desire to wield that power. The resulting pressure gradually compels the previously autocratic government to undertake democratic reforms.

In the 1990s, with the rise of genuine democracy in places like South Korea and Taiwan, however, those earlier assumptions giving capitalism all the credit for overcoming Asian autocracy appeared inadequate. No doubt capitalism did contribute to the growth of pluralistic institutions in Asia, just as it had done in Europe. But the seed of democracy had to fall on fertile ground before it could take root and grow. That fertile ground, in turn, was prepared by cultural and historical forces which have greatly influenced the nature of the emergent democracies. The evolution of democratic institutions in post-war Japan, for example, has been profoundly affected by Japanese social values and political history (including feudalism). The outcome is a form of democracy unique to Japan, yet still a democracy.

In the case of all of those countries in East Asia shaped by Confucianism – Taiwan, South Korea, and Japan – there are many contributing influences to a potentially successful democratic polity. One of the most important is the deep respect for education that permeates all Confucian societies. In a pre-industrial society, only a relatively small proportion of the population was able to become educated. This was also true in Europe. As Asia became industrialized, however, the size of the educated public grew dramatically. Assuming John Dewey was right in postulating a close correlation between education and democracy, this expansion of the educated public was as crucial for Asia as it was for Europe and America. The greater the number of educated citizens in a polity, the higher the level of public discourse; the higher the level of public discourse, the greater the chances for the success of democracy. In this respect, moreover, East Asia might be well positioned for the future both economically and politically. Its respect for education, which is arguably more developed there than in any other region of the world, is ideal for a future knowledge-based economy and democratic self-government. Indeed, Americans may have much to learn from the Asian example, particularly as public support for both secondary and higher education in the United States appears to be eroding.

This is not to say that the Chinese or Koreans or Japanese are natural revolutionaries, or even that they are egalitarian. In fact they are unabashedly elitist, clearly believing that only educated and morally upright individuals are qualified to serve in public office. But are these views so different from the assumptions of the founders of American or even Greek democracy? After all, Thomas Jefferson also believed, as we have noted above, that only a small percentage of a given population was qualified for participation in public affairs. The classical Athenians excluded not only women but also slaves and foreigners. The fact that Chinese did not historically elect their public officials through universal suffrage does not mean that their cultural values were fundamentally alien to the temper of modern democracy. If the experience of the East Asian democracies tells us anything, it is that democracy is part of a vast network of interlocking and interactive forces. Those forces are always changing, but they represent the expression of a universal impulse to be free.

Notes

1 'Democracy's Third Wave,' in Larry Diamond and Marc F. Plattner, eds, *The Global Resurgence of Democracy* (Baltimore: Johns Hopkins University Press, 1996), p. 21.
2 *Mencius*, Lau translation, 7B14, vol. II: 291.
3 *Mencius*, Lau translation, 4B3, vol. I: 159.

Further reading

General

For a clear exposition of the contribution of capitalism to the growth of democratic institutions in East Asia, see Samantha F. Ravich, *Marketization and Democracy: East Asian Experiences* (New York: Cambridge University Press, 2000). Daniel A. Bell's *East Meets West: Human Rights and Democracy in East Asia* (Princeton: Princeton

University Press, 2000) uses an effective device of conversational dialogue to explore Asian and Western values. For a fascinating collection of essays by the dean of American scholars on Confucianism, see Wm. Theodore De Bary's *Asian Values and Human Rights: A Confucian Communitarian Perspective* (Cambridge, MA: Harvard University Press, 1998). For an excellent collection of conference papers on a Confucian understanding of human rights, see Wm. Theodore De Bary and Tu Wei-ming, eds., *Confucianism and Human Rights* (New York: Columbia University Press, 1998). Thomas A. Metzger's pamphlet entitled *The Western Concept of the Civil Society in the Context of Chinese History* (Stanford: Hoover Institute Press, 1998) is a worthwhile introduction. See also Alan T. Wood's *Limits to Autocracy: From Sung Neo-Confucianism to a Doctrine of Political Rights* (Honolulu: University of Hawai'i Press, 1995).

South Korea

For a discussion on Korean political culture from the perspective of a social scientist, see Gail Helgesen, *Democracy and Authority in Korea: The Cultural Dimension in Korean Politics* (New York: St. Martin's, 1998). Ilpyong J. Kim and Young Whan Kihl's edited study, *Political Change in South Korea* (New York: Paragon House, 1988) is dated but still useful. For Korean politics see Hagen Koo, ed., *State and Society in Contemporary Korea* (Ithaca: Cornell University Press, 1994); and John Kie-Chiang Oh, *Korean Politics: The Quest for Democratization and Economic Development* (Ithaca: Cornell University Press, 1999). Kenneth Wells' *South Korea's Minjung Movement: The Culture and Politics of Dissidence* (Honolulu: University of Hawai'i Press, 1995) contains scholarly articles on populist nationalism in Korea. Doh C. Shin's *The Democratization of Mass Politics and Culture in Korea: The Korean Experience in Comparative Perspective* (Cambridge: Cambridge University Press, 1999) is an excellent study of political culture in Korea.

Taiwan

For a detailed and balanced appraisal of the significant elections in Taiwan in the 1990s, see John Franklin Copper, *Taiwan's Mid-1990s Elections: Taking the Final Steps to Democracy* (Westport: Praeger, 1998). Tun-jen Cheng and Stephan Haggard's edited volume, *Political Change in Taiwan* (Boulder: Lynne Rienner, 1992), although dated, contains valuable studies on the changes in the 1980s. The authoritative study of the politics of the transition to democracy in Taiwan is Linda Chao and Ramon H. Myers, *The First Chinese Democracy: Political Life in the Republic of China on Taiwan* (Baltimore: Johns Hopkins University Press, 1998). Hung-mao Tien and Steve Tsang's edited volume entitled *Democratization in Taiwan: Implications for China* (New York: St. Martin's Press, 1999), together with Tien's *Taiwan's Electoral Politics and Democratic Transition: Riding the Third Wave* (Armonk: M.E. Sharpe, 1996), contain valuable studies on selected topics. Alan M. Wachman's *Taiwan: National Identity and Democratization* (Armonk: M.E. Sharpe, 1994) provides a mid-1990s perspective. For a comparison of the Chinese and Taiwan experiences, see Bruce J. Dickson, *Democratization in China and Taiwan: The Adaptability of Leninist Parties* (New York: Oxford University Press, 1997). For a short introduction to democratization in Taiwan, see Jaushieh Joseph Wu, *Taiwan's Democratization: Forces Behind the New Momentum* (Hong Kong: Oxford University Press, 1995). For a useful collection of conference papers see Thomas J. Bellows, ed., *Taiwan and Mainland China: Democratization, Political Participation, and Economic Development in the 1990s* (Jamaica, NY: Center of Asian Studies, St. John's University, 2000).

China

Andrew J. Nathan's *Chinese Democracy* (Berkeley: University of California Press, 1985) is one of the best overall introductions to the subject by the leading specialist in the field. For a collection of essays by one of the central intellectual figures in the Chinese democracy movement, see David Bachman and Dali L. Yang, *Yan Jiaqi and China's Struggle for Democracy* (Armonk: M.E. Sharpe, 1991), and *Toward a Democratic China: The Intellectual Autobiography of Yan Jiaqi*, trans. David S.K. Hong and Denis C. Mair (Honolulu: University of Hawai'i Press, 1992). Roger V. Des Forges, Lou Ning, and Wu Yen-bo, eds, *Chinese Democracy and the Crisis of 1989: Chinese and American Reflections* (Albany: State University of New York Press, 1993) contains a variety of essays on the process of democratization in China. Edmund S.K. Fung's *In Search of Chinese Democracy: Civil Opposition in Nationalist China, 1929–1949* (Cambridge: Cambridge University Press, 2000) covers the democracy movement during the Republican era. Merle Goldman's *Sowing the Seeds of Democracy in China: Political Reform in the Deng Xiaoping Era* (Cambridge, MA: Harvard University Press, 1994) is an excellent source for democracy in post-Mao China. David L. Hall and Roger T. Ames have written a fascinating book of reflections on Chinese and Western views on human rights in *The Democracy of the Dead: Dewey, Confucius, and the Hope for Democracy in China* (Chicago: Open Court, 1999). For the best short introduction to Chinese law and its relation to Chinese culture, see Laszlo Ladany, *Law and Legality in China* (Honolulu: University of Hawai'i Press, 1992). *China's Search for Democracy: The Student and Mass Movement of 1989*, edited by Suzanne Odgen, Kathleen Hartford, Lawrence Sullivan, and David Zweig (Armonk: M.E. Sharpe, 1992), is a wonderful collection of documents pertaining to the 1989 demonstrations in Tiananmen Square. Anyone who doubts the courage and passion for freedom expressed by the students in the Tiananmen demonstrations should read *Cries for Democracy: Writings and Speeches from the 1989 Chinese Democracy Movement*, edited by Han Minzhu and Hua Sheng (Princeton: Princeton University Press, 1990). For an excellent report on the pace of village election reform in China, see Anne F. Thurston, *Muddling Toward Democracy: Political Change in Grassroots China* (Washington, DC: US Institute of Peace, 1998). Suisheng Zhao has compiled an excellent collection of studies on various topics in *China and Democracy: Reconsidering the Prospects for a Democratic China* (London: Routledge, 2000). See also Baogang He, *The Democratization of China* (London: Routledge, 1996).

Chapter 5

Later democracies in Southeast Asia

Thailand, Malaysia, Singapore, and Indonesia

Thailand

History

The Thai are descendents of a people who once lived in what is now northern Vietnam, southern China, and northeastern Laos. They migrated into present-day Thailand (known until 1939 as Siam) between the seventh and the thirteenth centuries. The first kingdom was at Sukhothai, which lasted from 1238 to 1350, after which they founded the kingdom of Ayutthaya north of present-day Bangkok. In the eighteenth century the Thais moved their capital to Bangkok and in 1782 the Thai throne was occupied by King Rama I, the first in the line of royalty that has lasted to the present day in Thailand.

During the golden age of European colonialism in the nineteenth century, Thailand was the only country in South and Southeast Asia to retain full sovereignty. There were two principal reasons for this. One was its location as a buffer between the French sphere of influence in Vietnam, Laos, and Cambodia, and the British sphere of influence in Malaya and Burma. The Thais paid a high price for freedom, however. They were forced to cede control of Cambodia and Laos to the French and portions of Malaya to the British. The second reason for Thai success in retaining independence was leadership. Two kings in particular stand out in terms of their openness to the West, their commitment to modernizing their country, and their wisdom in dealing with the Europeans: King Mongkut (Rama IV), who ruled from 1851 to 1868 (and was memorialized for American audiences in *The King and I*); and his son King Chulalongkorn (Rama V), who ruled from 1868 to 1910.

The twentieth century has been turbulent in terms of politics in Thailand. In 1932 the monarchy lost power, though not its position, to a shifting coalition of military and political leaders who rotated in and out of power for decades. From then until the present, Thailand has been a constitutional monarchy. It was one of the first countries in Asia to grant universal male and female suffrage.[1] In the decades immediately following the end of the Second World War, the region passed through a tumultuous period punctuated by wars of independence from European colonial powers as well as conflicts with indigenous communist movements. The Thai military often used the resulting instability as an excuse to seize power.

During this period, there were periodic movements for more democratic rights, often led by students and frequently resulting in violence against them by the government. There were as well occasionally democratic elections, such as those that took place in 1969. But they were usually short-lived, and followed, as in 1971, by military coups that suspended the former constitution. These coups were then followed by more student riots. From 1973 to 1976, there existed a short period of what might be called democratic rule. It failed, however, to establish economic and political stability, and was ended by yet another military coup. In 1988 a civilian government came to power that lasted until 1991 when the military once again attempted to take over the government, allegedly to root out the corruption that had plagued the previous government but primarily to reclaim their own control over the country. This time, however, the public reacted with huge demonstrations in the streets in 1992. Democratic values appear to have taken root among the population to a far greater degree than the military had realized. Indeed, the public reaction to the military coup was so widespread and intense that the position of the government soon became untenable, especially after it resorted to force to suppress the demonstrations, killing hundreds of people. At this point the king intervened and aligned the monarchy solidly behind democratic rule. The subsequent governments in the 1990s were civilian, but not notably more stable than before due to constantly shifting coalitions of political parties. Meanwhile, Thai society became increasingly pluralistic as the military refrained from direct rule (though it continued to play an influential role in the background). In 1997 a new constitution was promulgated that instituted sweeping reforms of the entire political structure of Thailand.

Institutions

In contrast with most other Asian democracies, Thailand has never had a dominant party.[2] Coalitions of parties shifted in response to changing issues and personalities. It has also never experienced the traumatic inequalities of colonial occupation or the devastation of civil war, as have all its neighbors in Southeast Asia in the twentieth century. This continuity with the past gives Thai society an underlying stability in terms of its basic institutions that bodes well for the future of democracy. One of the most important of those institutions had been the monarchy. Although King Bhumipol Adulyadej (who is the grandson of King Chulalongkorn, and ascended the throne in 1946) is only a constitutional monarch with no formal political power, he has acquired enormous respect among his people through his integrity and compassion for the welfare of his subjects. In what can only be seen as a delicious irony (for those who assume that monarchs are auto-matically against democracy), he has intervened during several crises to promote democratic forces and restrain the military, in 1973, 1981, and in 1992.

To be sure, not all traditional Thai habits and institutions are democratic in their basic orientation. Thailand has traditionally been ruled by a small elite drawn from three primary institutions: the bureaucracy, the military, and business. There is a long heritage of bureaucratic rule in Thailand, and of centralizing power into the hands of officials in the capital and away from the provinces. Thai society, moreover, is characterized by the prevalence of patron–client relationships at all levels of a kind that Robert Putnam talks about as having a dampening effect on democratic institution in southern Italy.[3] Those institutions, taken as a whole, form the backdrop to the remark-able changes that took place in the last decade of the century.

The most significant of those changes were the constitutional reforms of 1997, which were embodied in a document of 171 pages of detailed provisions. For the first time, members of the Senate were elected directly by the people. Another clause in the new constitution provided that, whereas in the past all local officials had been appointed by the central government, now they were to be elected by the local constituency. All in all, these reforms were intended to set Thai politics in a more hopeful direction, making politicians more accountable and responsive to the public, reducing the power of the civil bureaucracy to make policy, eliminating corruption, enhancing the role of local government while reducing the role of the central government, and stabilizing the national government.

There was much work to be done. The history of elections in Thailand has been spotty. An election held in March 1992 was widely regarded as being so tainted by vote-buying as to cast doubt on the validity of the outcome. On the other hand, the election that was held in the fall of the same year is thought to have been among the most fair in Thai history. Elections held after the constitutional reforms of 1997 have also been widely respected in terms of their fairness, with some exceptions. The 2001 elections resulted in the defeat of many politicians who had been widely suspected of corruption and vote-buying. But the new world of Thai politics is full of the ghosts of the past. Accusations of money politics continue to be made, especially after the wealthiest businessman in Thailand, Thaksin Shinawatra, was elected prime minister in 2001 amid charges of tax evasion that were later dis-missed. His vast wealth was in large part accumulated by exploiting a cozy relationship between his companies and the government. His rise to political power, moreover, was supported by the business community and by the banking industry, who received a bailout as soon as the new prime minister took office. It is not altogether clear, therefore, that big money has lost its power in Thai politics, but there is no question that it is losing many of its previous advantages.

In the past, one of the means by which the military exerted influence in Thailand was through their control of numerous radio and television stations, which may explain why the print media in Thailand have been notably more independent than radio and television. Until 1997, when the new constitution was adopted, the military controlled more than 200 radio stations and two television stations. That control has since been significantly reduced, opening up access to the electronic media to a much wider spectrum of political opinion. According to provisions of the 1997 Constitution, the government is enjoined to decentralize the electronic media and deregulate the telecommunications industry. Though their success has been incomplete due to the lingering resistance of many in the military, business, and government anxious not to lose their special privileges, the overall direction is positive.

A most dramatic instance of the feistiness of the newspapers in Thailand occurred in 1992. In that year the government, having presided over a widely discredited election (mentioned above) in which the military consolidated control over the country, used force to suppress public demonstrations against its legitimacy during the month of May. On May 17, in violation of a government decree, the English-language newspaper *The Nation* published a photograph of police officers clubbing a helpless protester. The resulting public outrage brought tens of thousands of citizens into the streets, precipitating the downfall of the government. By the end of the 1990s, the print media in Thailand, along with their counterparts in the Philippines, were widely regarded as the freest in Southeast Asia, though in the early years of the twenty-first century they still encountered numerous attempts to control them by a government notably sensitive to criticism.[4]

Thailand has seen the rise of new interest groups that express the diverse attitudes of the growing middle class. The new constitution contains numerous provisions protecting the right of the general population to organize for all kinds of political purposes, including initiating legislation and impeaching sitting politicians. It is one thing, of course, to legislate, quite another to implement. Labor unions, for example, remain relatively powerless. No more than 5 percent of the workforce is unionized, and most of those are confined to one company. Nevertheless, the new document goes a long way in establishing principles against which politicians and bureaucrats can be held accountable. Most observers remain cautiously optimistic regarding the evolution of Thai political institutions in the decade of the 1990s.

Conditions

Some have argued that the political culture of Thailand – and perhaps all of Southeast Asia – is not favorable to democracy because of a long tradition of deference to authority and a persistent structure of hierarchical social relations. Here as elsewhere, however, democratic roots have begun to sink down into the soil of Thai society. There has been a significant rise in the number and variety of non-governmental organizations (NGOs) active in promoting social and political causes, including grass-roots organizations by farmers, environmentalists, and promoters of urban renewal and community development.

In 1997, for example, a movement of local farmers known as the Assembly of the Poor marched on Bangkok and staged a three-month demonstration in front of Government House that eventually won a number of concessions from the government. In the same year an Association of Rural Doctors managed to protest successfully to reform the system for purchasing medicine and medical supplies in Thailand. At the same time, there are no radical movements in Thai society that offer an alternative vision of politics (the Thai Communist Party having become essentially irrelevant by the early 1980s).[5]

Another sign of progress is the gradual withdrawal of the military from direct involvement in politics. For more than two-thirds of the time since the overthrow of the monarchy in 1932, Thailand has been ruled by the military. Those days are probably over. Changes in political culture are having their effect on practical affairs, including growing support for civilian control of the military. With every passing year in which the military stay out of direct interference in political affairs, the principle of civilian control becomes increasingly entrenched. As the military becomes more professional, it becomes less susceptible to corruption and to interference in politics. There remains much to be done, as informal influence remains strong. But there are grounds for optimism.

The overall security of the state contributes to the reduced role of the military as well. The region of Southeast Asia was tormented by war for several decades of the last half of the twentieth century. These wars that plagued Thailand's neighbors during the 1960s and 1970s grew out of the various independent struggles waged by nationalistic groups seeking the expulsion of the European colonial powers of France (from Vietnam, Laos, and Cambodia), Britain (from Malaya and Burma), and the Netherlands (from Indonesia). Now that the wars are over, the region has been able to focus its resources more effectively on economic development.

There is no question but that the prosperity of the Thai economy in the past few decades has also fostered conditions favorable to the growth of democratic government in Thailand. One of those significant conditions has been the expansion of the middle class, which in 1996 was estimated to comprise one-fifth of the working population.[6] As the middle class expanded, so did literacy, travel, educational opportunities, and a press increasingly open and critical of government policies. It is wise to remember, however, that a group of people as large as 'the middle class' will contain a wide diversity of views and interests, not all of them equally favorable to democracy. Many scholars have noted that there is a strong desire at all levels of Thai society for order and stability, which under some circumstances manifests itself as support for authoritarian rule. The struggle between these contending expectations is itself, of course, part of the maturing process of democracy, and on balance a healthy phenomenon as long as it can find expression in constructive debate.

Thailand is also diverse in its ethnic makeup, containing a wide assortment of different ethnic groups, of which the most significant group is Chinese. Some observers estimate that 10 percent of the Thai population is of Chinese ancestry. Whatever their numbers, they control a percentage of the Thai economy out of all proportion to their numbers. Indeed, ethnic Chinese appear to dominate the Thai economy. One study done in the 1970s estimated that ethnic Chinese 'owned 90% of commercial and manufacturing assets, and half the capital of the banks.'[7] Individual examples abound. The largest corporate empire in Thailand is run by Dhanin Chearavanont, the son of Chinese immigrants. Ethnic Chinese have also entered politics (in contrast to their counterparts in Malaysia). The prime minister elected in 2001, Thaksin Shinawatra, who made a vast fortune in the telecommunications industry, is ethnic Chinese. This lopsided success, however, has not caused an undue amount of tension. Chinese appear to have been successfully integrated into Thai society, so that the conflicts that appear in Malaysia and Indonesia between ethnic Chinese and the indigenous population are largely absent in Thailand. The cultural trait of tolerance so often remarked upon by visitors to Thailand may have played a role in producing this atmosphere of cooperation.

An overall assessment of the prospects for democracy in Thailand is not easy. There is no shortage of pessimists who argue that the outward progress conceals underlying obstacles – such as endemic corruption – that will take a long time to remove and that cast doubt on the theory that a growing middle class fosters democracy. These pessimists argue that since modernization in Asian economies has been led by the state, the middle class is inclined to see a paternalistic state as its friend not its adversary. Furthermore, a tradition of deference to authority, encouraged by an educational system that emphasizes rote learning rather than critical thinking, does little to foster democratic values. Modern economic development has also brought with it greater inequalities in Thai society, in which 60 percent of the population possess only 25 percent of the nation's wealth.[8]

On the other hand, there are also many optimists, who tend to lend greater credence to the proliferation of pluralistic institutions that have already strengthened civil society in Thailand and curbed the power of the military on numerous occasions. They are also heartened by the growing openness of Thai society, the continuing growth in economic prosperity for the middle class, the absence of strong ethnic or religious divisions in Thai society, and the increasing ties between civil culture and political reform in Thailand. Which of these two very different views of democracy in Thailand will prevail only the future can tell. One thing is for sure: in Thailand as in every society the natural tension between freedom and equality is unavoidable and provides an everlasting challenge for even the most gifted leaders to find an appropriate balance.

Malaysia
History

Thailand's neighbor to the south, Malaysia, has had a very different experience in spite of its close proximity. Whereas Thailand was spared colonization by European powers, almost every aspect of Malaysia's political and social life has been profoundly affected by its colonial experience. Present-day Malaysia (known until the recent past as Malaya) was originally inhabited by ethnic Malay peoples who formed their own kingdoms and fell under the occasional political control of states centered in the island archipelago to its south during the first millennium AD. Over the centuries, traders from India brought Hinduism and Buddhism, which merged with local traditions to create a flourishing society well-integrated with the larger trading networks of Southeast Asia. Muslim influence arrived with the Arab traders beginning in the thirteenth century and added to the rich cultural diversity of the region.

The founding of Malacca around 1400 on the west coast of Malaya proved a turning point in Malaysian history. This city rapidly became one of the most cosmopolitan centers of international trade in the world, containing up to 15,000 traders from all over the Asian and Middle Eastern world and marking a significant increase in the influence of Islam in Malaysian life, though it was not until the nineteenth century that it became dominant. Portuguese traders arrived in the beginning of the sixteenth century and under their control the city declined. Malacca's fortunes were not improved when the Dutch took over in the middle of the seventeenth century.

It was the arrival of the British in the late eighteenth century that profoundly changed the history of the region now known as Malaysia. Although their original intention was to counter French influence in the Indian Ocean, the British soon discovered the economic potential of the Malay tin mines and rubber trees. Accordingly they established a complex plantation system to produce rubber and fruit, and imported large numbers of Chinese and Indians to work on the plantations and in the mines. To bring products to markets they constructed a transportation system, and to insure political stability they developed a complex arrangement of ruling through the indigenous Malay rulers known as sultans. In order to train local administrators they instituted an educational system based on English (as they had done in India and Burma and Hong Kong). The net effect of all these changes was to lay the foundation for the ethnic diversity (and tensions) of present-day Malaysia.

Unlike the French and the Dutch, against whom nationalist leaders in Southeast Asia had to wage war in order to gain independence, the British granted independence peacefully to Malaya in 1957. The only violence during the years leading up to (and for three years after) independence was provoked by a communist insurgency led primarily by ethnic Chinese. In 1963, Malaya joined with Sarawak and Sabah (on the northern rim of the island of Borneo) and Singapore to form a federation known as Malaysia. Nine hereditary sultans were joined into a constitutional monarchy that remains in effect today, in which the head of state rotates every five years among the sultans whose power is almost entirely ceremonial and symbolic. In 1965, Singapore objected to the dominance of Malays over Chinese in the government, resulting in its secession from the federation to become an independent city-state.

The system of government was modeled on the British parliamentary form, with a prime minister subject to an elected legislature consisting of a Senate and a House of Representatives. The first prime minister was the widely respected Tunku Abdul Rahman, whose commitment to democracy during his tenure in office from 1957 to 1970 was a major factor in its eventual success. In 1981 Mahathir bin Mohamad was elected prime minister and remained in office through four national elections, dominating Malaysian politics in the 1980s and 1990s and presiding over two decades of remarkable economic growth.

Institutions

Malaysia's experiment with democracy differs from that of its neighbor Thailand in at least one significant respect. In Thailand, parties have played a minor role in politics. In Malaysia, however, politics has been dominated by one major party since independence in 1957. This party, now called the United Malays National Organization (UMNO), reflects the underlying reality of Malaysia's multi-ethnic society. Slightly over half of Malaysia's population are Malay, slightly over one-third are ethnic Chinese, and about 10 percent are Indian. The need from the very beginning of the country's existence to mediate tensions between these groups led Tunku Abdul Rahman to forge a compromise that enabled the Malays to dominate politics while the Chinese dominated the economy.

When that compromise broke down in 1969 as a result of resentment by Chinese who felt disenfranchised, riots ensued that killed about two hundred people. The confluence of instability in the region (the war in Vietnam was at its height) and domestic disorder produced such concern in Malaysia that the government imposed martial law for almost two years. In 1971 the government proclaimed a New Economic Policy designed to improve the economic situation of the Malay population and stimulate the economy. The decades of remarkable economic growth that followed seemed to fortify the government's decision, though the power of the democratic opposition parties waned. Mahathir became prime minister in 1981 and set about to neutralize opposition to his rule among the various sectors of Malaysian politics. To a large extent he has succeeded, while retaining the structural components of democracy.

The government is led by officials who are elected in free and frequent elections. The constitution has never been revoked (in contrast to many of Malaysia's neighbors) and national elections have been held every five years, without fail, since independence. Whether those elections are fair may be open to debate. In practice only one party – UMNO – has a reasonable chance of winning a majority of seats in the legislature. To be sure, there exist opposition parties, and those parties do occasionally defeat candidates who represent the dominant party. But they have little to no chance of ever becoming a majority party. The real struggle for power in Malaysian politics thus takes place within the factions of the dominant party itself. To some degree this situation is a consequence of the larger context of ethnic divisions in Malaysian society, in which the political parties are organized along ethnic and not ideological lines. Since UMNO represents the Malays, who are the dominant majority, it is very difficult for a minority party to take over, or even for a coalition of parties to succeed.

Freedom of expression is much more curtailed in Malaysia than in Thailand. Most media outlets – newspapers, radio and television stations – are owned by political parties, who can hardly be expected to criticize themselves. A multitude of topics, especially those dealing with ethnic conflicts, are off limits. Mahathir has managed to muzzle the press in numerous ways, so that the newspapers are generally unwilling to criticize the government, since by doing so they would risk being banned. For its part, the government claims that these restrictions are necessary to preserve public order in the context of the country's deep ethnic divisions.

The opening up of Malaysia to the world economy, the undeniable success of the government in building an effective educational system that has catapulted the literacy rate into the ninetieth percentile, the advent of the Internet that brings the full range of global information to anyone with a computer and a modem, have all given the Malaysian middle class access to alternative sources of information to a degree never before possible. Over time, that access is bound to undermine the government's monopoly on the media, and expose it to criticism that it can no longer control. How long it will be before that process manifests itself in democratic politics remains to be seen.

The ability of groups to organize in Malaysia for political purposes is likewise curtailed by the government. Freedom of assembly can be exercised only within strict limits set by the government, including police permits for meetings of more than five people. Labor organizations face government restrictions on many fronts. Any organizations that might be associated with ethnic or religious differences face almost certain government interference with their freedom of association. Under the provisions of the Internal Security Act of 1960, the police may detain anyone they deem to have acted 'in a manner prejudicial to the security of Malaysia.'[9] Citizenship, on the other hand, is inclusive.

Conditions

The essential conditions for the flourishing of democracy in Malaysia are largely in place. There is not a single instance in the country's history since independence of the military or police intervening in political affairs as they have done in so many of Malaysia's neighbors. In that respect, democracy in Malaysia has developed deep and firm roots. In terms of democratic beliefs and political culture, the picture is more complicated. There is no question but that there is widespread support for democratic institutions in the general population. On the other hand, many in the middle class believe that in order to promote ethnic harmony and economic growth it is necessary to limit – to some degree – the civil liberties of the nation's citizens. Order takes precedence over democracy when the two seem in conflict with each other. As long as the government continues to be responsive to the needs of the various ethnic groups, and as long as the economy continues to flourish, there is little likelihood that such a civic compact will be challenged.

One other criterion for the success of democratic institutions – the absence of foreign control – is clearly in place. After the British granted independence to Malaya in 1957, they have remained uninvolved with Malaysian affairs in any way other than as an interested party with no special powers of any kind. One of their legacies, a well-trained judiciary, has been another source of stability in Malaysian society. Though its independence has been to some extent compromised by Mahathir's tendency to browbeat judges, even firing them when they don't rule in favor the government's wishes, the legal system is one of the stabilizing forces in modern Malaysian life.

Favorable conditions for democracy in Malaysia, as outlined above, include the stunning growth in the Malaysian economy over the past several decades, and the opening of Malaysian society to the world in terms of travel, education, trade, and communications. Looming over the whole question of democratic institutions, however, is the challenge of Malaysia's ethnic diversity and the tensions that have dominated the relationship among the various Malay, Chinese, Indian, and indigenous peoples. The former conditions favor democratic institutions, the latter authoritarian institutions, prompting one scholar to remark that 'the political regime in Malaysia is neither fully democratic nor fully authoritarian but contains elements of both.'[10] The relationship between these two poles is dynamic and mutually interactive. For example, the existence of opposition parties insures that the interests of Chinese and Indian and indigenous minorities are paid attention to by the government. Mahathir has performed a delicate balancing act over the decades of his tenure as prime minister. When he departs the scene, it is difficult to predict what will happen.

Singapore
History

Singapore began its existence a thousand years ago as a trading outpost for various states in the region. Its very name, derived from the Indian Sanskrit term 'Lion City' (*singhapura*), is testimony to its cosmopolitan origins. It derived its value by its location on an island adjacent to one of the major shipping lanes of the world between the southern coast of Malaya and the northern coast of Indonesia. All ships transiting between the South China Sea and the Indian Ocean pass by Singapore. After the emergence of Malacca as a trading center in the fifteenth century, Singapore declined into little more than a fishing village and hangout for pirates. Its present rise to fame began when Sir Thomas Stamford Raffles of the British East India Company took possession of the island in 1819. During most of the nineteenth and early twentieth centuries it formed a part of the British Straits Settlements. After the Second World War Great Britain granted it a provisional form of independence in 1959. In 1963, Singapore joined with Sabah, Sarawak, and Malaya to create the Republic of Malaysia. Conflicts arose immediately, however, over fears that Singapore's largely Chinese population (about three-quarters) would upset the Malay dominance of Malaysian politics. In 1965 Singapore separated from that union to become a fully independent city-state.

The leader of Singapore since the 1950s, and the architect of the city's astonishing economic growth during the last four decades of the twentieth century, has been Lee Kuan Yew. Prime minister from independence until he retired in 1990 (but continued to dominate politics from the sidelines) Lee presided over an extraordinarily successful system of government that combines the authoritarian and paternalistic traditions of Chinese governments of the past with the democratic forms of government developed in the modern world. When Lee stepped down, he was succeeded by his deputy Goh Chok Tong, who has carried on the same policies as his mentor. Singapore, with a population of more than 4 million in 2002, is universally regarded as one of the cleanest, safest, richest, and dullest cities in the world.

Institutions

The structure of government in Singapore is a parliamentary system of government in which officials are elected in free, fair, and frequent elections. Voting by all eligible citizens (with full male and female suffrage) is not only encouraged but compulsory. Corruption of the ballot box is virtually unheard of. Politicians are widely thought to be immune to the temptations of money and favoritism that are so common in other countries in Southeast Asia. They preside over a government bureaucracy widely considered to be among the most honest and efficient in the world.

On the other hand, the political system in Singapore can best be described as a one-party state. The People's Action Party (PAP) has dominated elections for the past four decades. There are opposition parties, but they have little chance of ever obtaining real power in parliament. In the fall elections of 2001, for example, the PAP won 82 out of 84 seats in parliament. The government achieves this feat by a variety of mechanisms. One is to curtail freedom of expression. The government owns all radio and television stations. Newspapers are closely tied to the PAP, and in effect censor themselves so that criticism of the government is allowed only within certain narrow limits. Foreign journals and magazines are banned whenever they publish articles deemed unduly critical of the government. Access to alternative sources of information, however, will undoubtedly be enhanced by access to the Internet, so this aspect of government control will become less crucial as more and more people surf the web.

Interest groups – especially if there is any ethnic component – are not looked upon favorably. They are quickly brought under the jurisdiction of government or PAP bureaucrats, with the result that there is very little associational autonomy. The Internal Security Act gives the government wide latitude in deciding whom to arrest and how long to detain them. Dissident social or political views are suppressed, and the government intrudes into people's lives to a significant degree: it is against the law to spit or even to fail to flush the toilet. The result is a city that is regimented to the point that the government is now becoming concerned that its most creative young people are leaving to escape the suffocating atmosphere of state control that prevails in the city-state.

Conditions

One of the strongest points in favor of democracy in Singapore is the complete absence of interference in politics by the military and police. Under Lee Kuan Yew, the civilian government has been in complete command of the coercive arm of the state. Neither has there been, ever since the departure of the British, any strong foreign control hostile to democracy. The rule of law prevails, and the judiciary is widely respected for its professionalism and honesty. How far it is willing to go to challenge the state is another question. There is no question as well that the forces of a modern market economy and society all favor the further development of democratic institutions in Singapore, as the middle class continues to grow in size and sophistication. Sub-cultural pluralism, the bane of Singapore's neighbor to the north, has been muted in Singapore, both by the level of prosperity accruing to all ethnic groups, and by policies of the government designed to mitigate ethnic divisions, such as requiring ethnic groups to live interspersed with each other (so that they will presumably understand each other better) rather than in ghettos.

Singapore's experience in government offers yet another variant of democracy that is different in significant ways from that of its neighbors in Southeast Asia. Singapore has managed to avoid the ethnic conflicts that prevail in Malaysia, the interference by the military that plague Thailand and Indonesia, while riding a wave of economic development that brought it from a condition of relative backwardness in the early 1960s to a level of per capita GDP in the 1990s that was higher than Western Europe's. At the same time, the government arrogated to itself such powers over every aspect of its citizens' lives as to call into question its commitment to the principle of popular sovereignty.

Its paternalistic and authoritarian dominance over Singaporean society was based upon an allegedly Confucian assumption that in times of crisis (and even in 'normal' times) an educated elite is better equipped to act in the public interest than the people themselves. That justification can be called into question on several grounds. First, the crises that have dominated the region in the past — communist insurgencies, wars of independence, ethnic conflicts, Singapore's relative economic backwardness — have abated if not completely disappeared. Second, Singapore's amazing economic growth has given rise to a highly educated middle class with a sophisticated understanding of politics. Third, other 'Confucian' democracies — such as Taiwan and South Korea — are far more open in their political processes than Singapore and have been notably successful. Fourth, Confucianism itself is more complex than the truncated version extolled by the Singaporean government. In fact Lee Kuan Yew is merely the most recent of a long line of Chinese rulers (including the present ones in China as well) who have twisted and distorted the Confucian tradition to justify their own imperial ambitions.[11] Given Lee's status in Singapore, and his refusal to follow the statesmanlike model of Chiang Ching-kuo in Taiwan and dismantle the authoritarian remnants of the past, very little real reform will be possible until he has departed the scene. The great irony of Lee's career is although he has been a great enemy of communism throughout his life, he used the power of the state to micro-manage almost every aspect of his citizens' lives. In engineering a society of enormous productive power, he has created a machine without a soul.

Indonesia

Indonesia is the fourth-largest country in the world in terms of population. Blessed with astonishing natural beauty and vast tropical forests, it is also spread out over almost 14,000 islands stretching 3,000 miles across the South China Sea. Approximately 88 percent of the population is Muslim, making it the largest Islamic nation in the world. The remainder is primarily Buddhist. Although the ethnic majority is Malay, the geographic expanse has fostered over time a wide variety of different ethnic communities. Such a large and diverse population on so many different islands makes fragmentation of purpose a major danger to national unity and a challenge to a stable democracy. On the other hand, one could make the case that only a sense of common purpose fostered by democratic practices of public participation in government is likely to promote a stable polity over the long haul. Indonesia is also an ideal case study for those who believe that one of the challenges facing the world in the next generation is to foster democracy in the Islamic world.

History

Indonesia has been a crossroads of human interaction from earliest times. Contact with India occurred very early, resulting in significant influence first of Hinduism then of Buddhism on the coastal areas of Indonesia. Settlers from the main islands of Indonesia not only migrated to the thousands of surrounding islands, but even ventured as far as the island of Madagascar off the southern coast of Africa, which was first settled by Austronesian peoples from Indonesia a thousand years ago. By the fifth century AD Indonesians were trading regularly with China. Although influences from the outside may have been important, Indonesians also had their own highly developed cultural traditions, borrowing from the outside only what they wanted. Distinctive cultural traits that have lasted to the present, such as *gamelan* music and *wayang* drama, were already in evidence two thousand years ago. The first major political state was Sri Vijaya on the island of Sumatra, which lasted for five centuries and relied on its spice trade with China – conducted by Indonesian merchants – for the revenue that sustained its political power. The cultural accomplishments of Sri Vijaya include the magnificent Buddhist temple complex of Borobudur, one of the great monuments of world architecture. The kingdom's power waned when Chinese traders began to sail in their own ships to the spice producers during the Song dynasty (960–1279), cutting out the Indonesian middlemen and in the process lowering state revenues.

The next high point was provided by the state of Majapahit in Java in the fourteenth century, which controlled considerable territory and also derived its revenue from profits from its trading network. Muslim influence, brought by Arab traders plying the monsoon winds of the Indian Ocean, began to have a significant impact on Indonesian life by the fifteenth century. Trading communities anxious to tap into the lucrative Arab trade found it expedient to themselves convert to Islam. In the process Islamic belief and practice were absorbed through the tolerant membrane of Indonesian culture, becoming an integral part of the existing social values.

Although the Portuguese were the first Europeans to arrive on the scene in the sixteenth century, it was the Dutch who transformed Indonesian political life, beginning with the formation of the Dutch East India Company in 1602. At first administering their commercial interests through existing Indonesian rulers, the Dutch gradually increased their presence and control over Indonesian life during the nineteenth century. The sale of Indonesian products became a major source of revenue for Holland.

The underlying purpose of Dutch rule was to exploit the resources of the region for the benefit of the Dutch treasury, but in the process they brought to the far-flung islands of the archipelago some sort of centralized administration, and thereby contributed in no small part to the eventual formation of a unified Indonesian state. In contrast to the British and American colonies, however, the Dutch made no effort to build effective educational institutions or to foster representative political bodies that could build habits of cooperation and compromise. The absence of these institutional aids to democracy was to have a long-term impact on Indonesian politics by encouraging leaders to rely on authoritarian rather than participatory solutions to problems.

In the 1920s a nationalist movement appeared that came to be led by a charismatic young engineer named Sukarno. When the Japanese occupied Indonesia in 1942, the nationalists saw an opportunity to rid themselves of Dutch rule, but soon realized that the Japanese were no more interested in promoting the welfare of Indonesians than the Dutch had been. When the war ended in 1945, Sukarno announced the independence of a new Indonesian state, which the Dutch resisted by force until they finally agreed to a declaration of an independent state of Indonesia in December 1949. In 1955 a relatively free and open election took place but stability was marred by the rise of regional interests as well as political factionalism within the government. In 1959, Sukarno preempted the constitutional processes and essentially took over full control of the government. After six years of disastrous economic policies, an attempted military coup in 1965 believed to have been promoted by Chinese communists released pent-up frustrations and precipitated a bloodbath in the country, largely against ethnic Chinese, resulting in half a million deaths.

Out of that confusion emerged a new leader, a military general by the name of Suharto. Sukarno was put under house arrest until his death in 1970. For the next thirty years Suharto presided over a state that can best be described as authoritarian. Toward the end of his rule popular resentment over widespread corruption among Suharto's family and friends grew more widespread, especially in the wake of the economic downturn beginning in 1997. In a remarkable expression of popular demand for democracy, widespread demonstrations in the streets, partly by students, reached a crescendo in 1998. When troops opened fire on student demonstrators, killing several hundred, demonstrators were only emboldened. Finally Suharto resigned as president and was succeeded by the vice-president, Bucharuddin Jusuf Habibie, whose brief tenure in office was followed by national elections widely considered the first fair and open elections in the history of the country.

Although Sukarno's daughter Megawati Sukarnoputri received the largest number of votes, she did not command a majority, and the People's Consultative Assembly elected Abdurrahman Wahid as president. A Muslim cleric and head of the largest Islamic organization in Indonesia, Wahid did not move decisively to deal with the major issues confronting the country, and gradually his support eroded amid confusion and corruption scandals implicating many of his own supporters. When the legislature voted to impeach him in 2000, he issued an order suspending the body, at which point the Consultative Assembly met and replaced him as president by Megawati in July 2001. The next round of national elections were scheduled for 2004, though many observers were concerned over signs that Megawati was cozying up to the military and bypassing normal channels of consultation.

Institutions

The great challenge to political institutions in Indonesia is in part built into the country's geography, which is so spread out across the ocean that the centrifugal force of fragmentation is very strong. In the past the government has followed a number of policies designed to overcome this inherent tendency to disunity. It has tried to develop an ideology of nationalism, to centralize the administrative and economic structure of the country in Java, and to concentrate economic development there as well in order to counteract the advantages other islands possessed due to their more abundant natural resources.[12] The presumption that unity is more important than efficiency and democracy is widespread among government bureaucrats, and it remains to be seen whether the new experiment in democracy will change that presumption. Some signs of improvement appeared in the early 2000s. In January, 2001, sweeping reforms were introduced that granted a great deal of autonomy to local governments at both the provincial and district levels.

Free elections in Indonesia took place in the 1950s before Sukarno seized power in 1959. Although Suharto called national elections periodically during his rule, they were carefully orchestrated and there were no viable opponents. Only after his resignation in 1998 did elections take place that can reasonably be said to have been fair and free. Their very novelty made it impossible to predict whether they would last. Nevertheless, the parliament in the early 2000s proceeded with a set of reforms that gave grounds for optimism.

In August, 2002, the People's Consultative Assembly approved a new series of amendments to take effect in 2004 that would remove the remaining seats reserved for the military in parliament. Along with a decision to make the police (insofar as they exist at all in some parts of the country) report to the civil government rather than the military, this action by the legislature was another important step in edging the military to the sidelines in Indonesian politics. There were also plans for a two-chamber legislature that would give regions a greater say in legislative issues and therefore address complaints that the national government is too highly centralized. The president, as of the 2004 election, will no longer be chosen by parliament but by popular vote.

One of Habibie's achievements was to remove government controls over the media in Indonesia, and they have responded with gusto (the other achievement being his decision to call the first free elections in Indonesia's history). Since 1998 Indonesia has enjoyed one of the most open and free presses in Southeast Asia. Alternative sources of information available to the Indonesian public have been similarly diverse. In terms of associational autonomy, once again the situation improved dramatically after the fall of Suharto. Now non-governmental organizations (NGOs) are pouring into the country along a whole range of interests from the environment to disease to poverty. Citizenship remains formally inclusive, though many ethnic Chinese complain that they are targeted for discrimination (and bribes) by government officials because of their ethnicity.[13]

Conditions

The military has played an important role in Indonesian politics. In a country so spread out over thousands of islands, it was in many places the only force for order. In order to pay for its upkeep in the early years, the military had been encouraged to invest in business ventures. The association of force and profit provided more opportunities for corruption than many generals were able to resist. To make matters worse, poorly trained and undisciplined troops sometimes exacerbated ethnic conflicts so that the overall impact of the military was often to undermine support for the state, and certainly not to inspire confidence in the government's commitment to democracy. On the other hand, in marked contrast with the experience of Thailand, in Indonesia the military has engineered a successful coup only once, when Suharto succeeded Sukarno in 1965. Since then it has been an effective tool of central government power. Politicians must seek its support, but in general it has not been able to suppress democratic forces from expressing their will.

Democratic beliefs and political culture in Indonesia are in their infancy, having only been allowed to develop in public since Suharto stepped down in 1998. On the other hand, there is no question that civic culture is growing. For this the government can take a great deal of indirect (and probably unintentional) credit. The nationalist ideology of *pancasila*, which, to be sure, was promoted by the state and designed to foster national unity and cohesion, nevertheless contained as one of its five elements the doctrine of democracy. In retrospect, Suharto could be said to have contributed to the rise of democracy in Indonesia, however indirectly. For one thing, he presided over the rise of the urban middle class (which eventually overthrew him). Whereas Sukarno had squandered the economic opportunities of a country rich in natural resources and cheap labor, Suharto turned the running of the economy over to a group of economists known as the 'Berkeley mafia' who had degrees from the University of California. Their policies of privatizing the industrial and service sectors and opening up the economy to global competition resulted in stunning levels of growth in the three decades of his rule. Education in the Suharto years also vastly improved. Under his rule literacy rates mushroomed from 40 to 90 percent.[14]

That said, it is also true that a rule of law was only partially implemented in Indonesia. The court system remained so corrupt that its effectiveness, and its reputation among the general public, was severely compromised. Until there are substantial reforms it cannot be relied upon to exercise restraint on the abuse of power by government officials. In the early 2000s, it still remains largely rule by the greased palm. In addition, the middle class is not uniformly in favor of democratic institutions, which many of them often associate with disorder and chaos. The elite and middle classes under Suharto were often benefiting so much from government policies that they were not necessarily in favor of democracy, causing one specialist to remark that in Indonesia 'most of the elite and middle class have little sympathy for liberal democracy.'[15]

Indonesia also faces considerable challenge just by virtue of the ethnic diversity of its peoples. Spread out over thousands of miles and thousands of islands, there are at least 200 separate languages spoken by Indonesians. There also exists a small minority of Chinese – about 3 percent – who nevertheless control a large portion of the country's economic wealth, some say up to 60 percent. This disproportionate ratio creates tensions between these communities that occasionally flare up into violent acts against the Chinese. Add to this ethnic mix regional loyalties and religious differences and it is small wonder that the ruling elite in the capital of Jakarta have been reluctant to permit the devolution of power required for a truly democratic process to take effect and capture the loyalty of the people at large. There is much room for pessimism. One close observer notes the overwhelming challenges, which include 'the geographic and ethnic fragmentation of the nation, economic inequalities (including Chinese dominance of the economy), uneducated and ignorant masses who are incapable of making informed political choices, the undeveloped economy, and the need to improve the people's welfare.'[16]

The role of Islam in all this mix remains unclear. According to one scholar, 'the major obstacle to democracy in Indonesia remains the place of

Islam.'[17] That perspective is countered by a recent study that concludes that Indonesia has the 'world's largest movement for a democratic and pluralist Islam.'[18] All in all, Indonesia remains a fascinating experiment – a work in progress – in the development of democratic institutions in a country facing significant economic and social as well as political challenges. The size and location of the country automatically confer a global significance to the outcome of the experiment, for which one can readily find evidence for both hope and despair simultaneously. For those who believe that it is vitally important for the future peace of the world to bring Islamic countries into the family of democratic nations, Indonesia may well play a pivotal role in world politics.

Notes

1 Clark D. Neher and Ross Marlay, *Democracy and Development in Southeast Asia: The Winds of Change* (Boulder: Westview Press, 1995), p. 29.
2 Neher and Marlay, ibid., p. 39.
3 *Making Democracy Work: Civic Traditions in Modern Italy* (Princeton: Princeton University Press, 1993).
4 John Girling, *Interpreting Development: Capitalism, Democracy, and the Middle Class in Thailand* (Ithaca: Cornell University Press, 1996), p. 66.
5 Girling, ibid., pp. 48–49.
6 Girling, ibid., p. 43.
7 *Economist* (July 18, 1992), p. 21.
8 Girling, op. cit., p. 78.
9 Neher and Marlay, op.cit., p. 107.
10 Harold Crouch, 'Malaysia: Neither Authoritarian Nor Democratic,' in *Southeast Asia in the 1990s: Authoritarianism, Democracy, and Capitalism*, ed. Kevin Hewison, Richard Robison, and Garry Rodan (St. Leonards, Australia: Allen and Unwin, 1993), p. 136.
11 For a more detailed discussion of this topic, see Alan T. Wood, *Limits to Autocracy: From Sung Neo-Confucianism to a Doctrine of Political Rights* (Honolulu: University of Hawai'i Press, 1995), especially the first chapter.
12 Bob Lowry, 'Indonesia: From Suharto to Democracy,' Discussion Paper #19 (Canberra: Australian National University, 1997), p. 22.
13 *The Straits Times* (in Singapore), May 22, 2002.
14 Hefner, op. cit., p. xii.
15 Bob Lowry, 'Indonesia: From Suharto to Democracy,' Discussion Paper #19 (Canberra: Australian National University, 1997), p. 16.
16 Ibid., p. 16.
17 Lowry, op. cit., p. 29.
18 Robert W. Hefner, *Civil Islam: Muslims and Democratization in Indonesia* (Princeton: Princeton University Press, 2000), p. 6.

Further reading

General

David Kelly and Anthony Reid's edited collection *Asian Freedoms: The Idea of Freedom in East and Southeast Asia* (New York: Cambridge University Press, 1998) has a number of excellent articles, as does Anek Laothamatas's *Democratization in Southeast and East Asia* (New York: St. Martin's, 1997) and Kevin Hewison, Richard Robison, and Garry Rodan's *Southeast Asia in the 1990s: Authoritarianism, Democracy and Capitalism* (Sydney: Allen and Unwin, 1993). For additional general treatments, see Clark D. Neher and Ross Marlay, *Democracy and Development in Southeast Asia: The Winds of Change* (Boulder: Westview Press, 1996); James W. Morley, ed., *Driven by Growth: Political Change in the Asia-Pacific Region* (Armonk: M.E. Sharpe, 1999); and Ian Marsh, Jean Blondel, and Takashi Inoguchi, eds, *Democracy, Governance, and Economic Performance: East and Southeast Asia* (Tokyo: United Nations University Press, 1999). An excellent collection of studies on civil society in Malaysia, Singapore, and Indonesia can be found in Robert W. Hefner, ed., *The Politics of Multiculturalism: Pluralism and Citizenship in Malaysia, Singapore, and Indonesia* (Honolulu: University of Hawai'i Press, 2001).

Thailand

For a classic introduction to Thai politics see John Girling's *Thailand: Society and Politics* (Ithaca: Cornell University Press, 1981), as well as his more recent *Interpreting Development: Capitalism, Democracy, and the Middle Class in Thailand* (Ithaca: Cornell Southeast Asia Program Publications, 1996). Kevin Hewison's excellent edited volume *Political Change in Thailand: Democracy and Participation* (London: Routledge, 1997) contains a wide variety of studies on specific topics in Thai politics. For an illuminating study of one of the main figures in Thai democracy, see David Van Praagh, *Thailand's Struggle for Democracy: The Life and Times of M.R. Seni Pramoj* (New York: Holmes and Meier, 1996). See also Anek Laothamatas's *Business Associations and the New Political Economy of Thailand: From Bureaucratic Polity to Liberal Corporatism* (Boulder: Westview Press, 1992).

Malaysia

For a good overall introduction to Malaysian government and politics see Harold Crouch's *Government and Society in Malaysia* (Ithaca: Cornell University Press, 1996). R.S. Milne and Diane K. Mauzy's *Politics and Government in Malaysia* (Vancouver: University of British Columbia Press, 1980), is a standard resource. For overviews of democracy in Malaysia, see Anne Munro-Kua, *Authoritarian Populism in Malaysia* (New York: St. Martin's Press, 1996) for her concept of 'authoritarian-populism'; Syed Farid Alatas, *Democracy and Authoritarianism in Indonesia and Malaysia: The Rise of the Post-colonial State* (New York: St. Martin's Press, 1997); and William Case, *Semi-Democracy in Malaysia: Pressures and Prospects for Change* (Canberra: Australian National University, 1992). Abdul Rahman Embong has written an excellent study on the rise of the Malaysian middle class entitled *State-led Modernization and the New Middle Class in Malaysia* (New York: Palgrave, 2002).

Singapore

For a solid assessment of Lee Kuan Yew's life and political thought, see Michael D. Barr's *Lee Kuan Yew: The Beliefs Behind the Man* (Washington, DC: Georgetown

University Press, 2000). Beng-Huat Chua's *Communitarian Ideology and Democracy in Singapore* (London and New York: Routledge, 1995) has a balanced interpretation of the political culture in Singapore. For an excellent collection of articles on Singapore, see Garry Rodan, ed., *Singapore* (Burlington, Vermont: Ashgate, 2001). For a pessimistic evaluation of democratic reform in Singapore, see E.C. Paul, 'Obstacles to Democratization in Singapore,' Working Paper #78 (Clayton, Australia: Centre of Southeast Asian Studies, 1992).

Indonesia

For a superbly written and extremely thoughtful challenge to the conventional wisdom that Islamic countries are resistant to democracy, see Robert W. Hefner, *Civil Islam: Muslims and Democratization in Indonesia* (Princeton: Princeton University Press, 2000). For valuable insight into the unifying role played by the national ideology of Pancasila, consult Douglas E. Ramage, *Politics in Indonesia: Democracy, Islam, and the Ideology of Tolerance* (New York: Routledge, 1995). For a comparative study of Malaysia and Indonesia, see Syed Farid Alatas, *Democracy and Authoritarianism in Indonesia and Malaysia: The Rise of the Post-Colonial State* (New York: St. Martin's, 1997). Anders Uhlin's *Indonesia and the 'Third Wave of Democratization': The Indonesian Pro-Democracy Movement in a Changing World* (New York: St. Martin's, 1997) is especially valuable. A good collection of articles on Indonesian democracy is David Bourchier and John Legge's *Democracy in Indonesia: 1950s and 1990s* (Victoria, Australia: Centre of Southeast Asian Studies, Monash University, 1994). For a more general collection of articles on modern Indonesian politics, see also David Bourchier and Vedi Hadiz, eds, *Indonesian Politics and Society: A Reader* (London: Routledge, 2002). A good general history is M.C. Ricklefs, *A History of Modern Indonesia Since c. 1200* (Palo Alto: Stanford University Press, 2002). For a review of modern government and politics, consult Adam Schwarz, *A Nation in Waiting: Indonesia's Search for Stability* (Boulder: Westview Press, 2000).

Chapter 6

Fragile democracies in South Asia

Pakistan, Bangladesh, and Sri Lanka

Pakistan

History

Although the nation of Pakistan did not come into formal existence until 1947, the year it was partitioned off from India to create a Muslim state, its roots lie in the previous centuries of the Mughal empire in India. The Mughals, descendants of Central Asian peoples (including the Mongols, from which they derived their name), had adopted the Islamic faith before their leader Babur conquered India in the sixteenth century. By the time the British assumed sovereignty over India in the middle of the nineteenth century, a significant minority of the Indian population had converted to Islam. In the early years of the Indian independence movement, Muslims and Hindus cooperated against a common adversary, but by the 1930s the Muslim community grew fearful that its interests would be ignored by the much larger Hindu majority. The voice of Muslims in India was largely expressed through the Muslim League headed by Muhammad Ali Jinnah who, like Mahatma Gandhi, had been educated as a lawyer in Britain. For decades a champion of cooperation between the Hindu and Muslim communities in India, by the early 1940s Jinnah had become convinced that the only solution for Muslims was to form two separate and independent states: a Muslim Pakistan and a secular (but largely Hindu) India.

The British government, after much hesitation, finally concurred. Independence was granted to Pakistan on August 14, 1947 (one day before India's independence). Pakistan itself was divided geographically into two areas separated by India: East Pakistan (now Bangladesh) with a population of largely Bengali Muslims, and West Pakistan, where the capital was located (originally in Karachi and then later in Islamabad), where ethnic Punjabis comprised 60 percent of the population and dominated the government and military. The process of Partition itself – with Muslims relocating west into the new state of Pakistan and Hindus relocating east into the new state of India – was violent and brutal. Widespread massacres of up to a million of these uprooted migrants took place on both sides, poisoning relations between India and Pakistan from the very beginning.

Unfortunately, Jinnah himself was gravely ill with tuberculosis, and died in 1948, depriving the young nation of the only leader able to play the same role that Jawaharlal Nehru did in India in terms of guiding the country through the first few years of democratic government. The only leader of remotely comparable stature, Liaqat Ali, was himself assassinated in 1951. The absence of competent and honest leadership in Pakistan has turned out to be a serious problem ever since.

In a pattern we have seen all too often in Southeast Asia, the military stepped into the void created by the lack of civilian leadership. After Ali's assassination, politics became more and more chaotic, until in 1958 General Muhammad Ayub Khan seized power and ruled for ten years. He oversaw a new constitution that created a National Assembly elected indirectly by an electoral college. After an unsuccessful war with India over Kashmir in 1965, support for Ayub faded away and he was succeeded by another general Agha Muhammad Yahya Khan, who proceeded to change yet again the makeup of the National Assembly. In the first truly national election in late 1970, which was based on the principle of one-person, one-vote, the more numerous Bengalis in East Pakistan had the advantage over the Punjabis in West Pakistan who had dominated the government since independence. When it became clear that the Punjabis would resist surrendering their power, East Pakistan decided to secede from the state of Pakistan and declare itself the independent state of Bangladesh. The Pakistani army, made up mostly of Punjabis, intervened to suppress the secession movement with such brutality that 10 million refugees fled into the neighboring Indian state of Bengal, eventually triggering an Indian military response in December 1971. In only two weeks the Pakistani army was defeated and compelled to surrender to India. East Pakistan promptly declared independence as the new state of Bangladesh. Yahya Khan resigned, and Zulfikar Ali Bhutto became the president of Pakistan, which now consisted only of the former West Pakistan.

Bhutto ruled from 1971 to 1977, presiding over a civilian government that promulgated yet another constitution providing for a bicameral legislature and a chief executive prime minister responsible (as in Great Britain) to the legislature. Bhutto implemented a socialist economic program that stifled entrepreneurial activity. Political factionalism under Bhutto grew so divisive that once again the military was provoked to intervene, this time under the auspices of Army Chief of Staff General Zia ul-Haq, whose kangaroo courts then tried Bhutto for murder and hanged him. Zia tried to cultivate support for his rule with the conservative Islamic community by such devices as creating a federal Sharia court and banning interest in banking investments. In 1988 he was killed in a plane crash that had all the earmarks of sabotage. No one was ever prosecuted.

What followed for the next decade was a revolving door of civilian governments run either by Benazir Bhutto (Zulfikar Ali Bhutto's daughter and the first woman to lead a modern Islamic state), or Nawaz Sharif. Both developed reputations for fostering corruption and proved unable to forestall outbreaks of domestic violence between ethnic and religious minorities within the country. In October 1999, Pervez Musharraf, the Army Chief of Staff, seized power in yet another military coup, promising to bring civilian government to the country through elections in October 2002 (which, though they did take place, did not appear to reduce Musharraf's power). Though earning international credibility through his cooperation with the United States against the Taliban in Afghanistan – who had come to power largely through Pakistani support – Musharraf set about consolidating his power by suppressing opposition to his rule and keeping the judicial branch subordinate to his will in the time-honored way of all his military predecessors. By tying his fortunes to the United States, moreover, he alienated his government from the conservative Islamic forces in Pakistan that previous military rulers had nurtured and supported. It remained to be seen whether those chickens would eventually come home to roost.

Institutions

The historical survey above does not provide much encouragement for those seeking evidence of democracy in Pakistan. Elected officials have been routinely shunted aside by the military. The first free and fair election took place in 1970, almost twenty years after independence, but resulted in the breakup of the country. The next election in 1977 was marked by so much fraud that the opposition parties refused to accept the results. Consequently, the military intervened once again allegedly to restore order. Reasonably fair elections took place in 1988 and 1990, but civilian politicians were unable to restore confidence in democratic institutions due to persistent reports of corruption.

Freedom of expression in Pakistan has passed through many different stages. In the years immediately following independence there was a reasonable degree of freedom, but after General Ayub Khan took over in 1958, curbs on the press were widespread and effective. Journalists and editors were arrested and their newspapers put under the administration of the government. Some relaxation under Bhutto in the 1970s was followed by more government repression under Zia in the late 1970s and through the 1980s. After Benazir Bhutto took over in 1988, the press has been able to reassert its natural role of holding the government accountable for its actions. Whether they will be able to maintain their freedoms under Musharraf is still unknown.

The main power-brokers in Pakistani society are the landowning elite, government bureaucrats, leaders of Islamic religious groups, and the military. All have contended with each other for power without much thought for the interests of the nation as a whole. In the words of one scholar, 'Pakistan, in its short history, has suffered at the hands of elitist bureaucrats, arrogant generals, opportunist feudalists, bigoted *mullahs* and a regionalized inter-mediate class.'[1] For civil society to grow and prosper, other interest groups must be allowed to form themselves and flourish. There are some favorable signs. One barometer of change is the growing ability of women to form associations that promote women's welfare across a whole spectrum of issues such as opening up new professions to women, and advocating for better pay, better working conditions, and more legal rights. During the 1990s, the growth of civic and business organizations outside the circle of government control has been a positive force for pluralism in Pakistan. Non-governmental organizations from abroad have also entered the mix, in spite of many efforts by the government to control or curtail the influence of some of them, particularly human rights organizations that focus on the abuses of power by government functionaries.

Conditions

The single greatest barrier to democracy in Pakistan is the disposition of the military to usurp power from civilian politicians. The *Economist*, with its characteristic flair for the pungent sentence, put it this way: 'The military in Pakistan is the problem to which it pretends to be the solution.'[2] For democratic beliefs and political culture to take root, they have to be nurtured both from below and above. Until the military generals agree to remain out of politics, even when leading politicians appear manifestly unable to govern effectively, Pakistan will find it impossible to make the transition to full democracy. With yet another military regime in power after 1999 in Pakistan, it is difficult to imagine that democratic values are going to be encouraged from above, in spite of the claims of President Musharraf.

Liberal democrats in Pakistan can only hope for a period of economic growth long enough and strong enough to cultivate an increasingly active middle class capable of defending its own interests and demanding greater transparency and accountability on the part of the government. That level of economic growth, however, requires stability, and the continuing cycle of violence and conflict between the various ethnic, religious, and regional groups in Pakistan does not bode well for the future of democracy in that troubled country. The larger context of disputes with India over Kashmir and with the fundamentalist Islamic Taliban in Afghanistan (with many supporters in Pakistan) only further complicates the issue by providing the government with yet another excuse to postpone democratic reforms, or to keep democratically elected politicians on a very short tether. The added uncertainty resulting from the American campaign in Afghanistan certainly does not improve the picture. Extremist Islamic groups, normally marginal-ized in a country where most of the population is religiously moderate, may be able to capitalize on a wide assortment of public resentments against the government to build up their own power.

Bangladesh

History

Bangladesh, as we have seen above, was formed from East Pakistan after a bitter and brutal war of independence with the Pakistani army in 1971 (aided by India). Bangladesh began life with several strikes against it. Its largely agricultural population was poorly educated, its industrial infrastructure was almost nonexistent, and its topography exposed it to frequent floods from the Ganges and Bramaputra Rivers and storms from the Bay of Bengal. Fortunately, it created a parliamentary form of government whose first prime minister, Sheikh Mujibur Rahman, had been the leader of the independence movement and widely popular in the country. His decision to emulate the socialist policies of his neighbor India did little to improve economic conditions, which were further undermined by a series of natural disasters in 1974 that wiped out most of the country's food supply. In 1975, he was assassinated during a military coup, after which an army general by the name of Ziaur Rahman emerged as the paramount leader and was elected to the presidency in 1978. In 1981 he himself was assassinated in an attempted coup. After a short democratic interlude, General Hossain Mohammad Ershad took over power in another military coup in 1982, and ruled by martial law until 1988, when he won an uncontested election as president. He resigned in the face of increasing public opposition to his rule in 1990.

In a pattern in South Asia by now familiar to readers, he was succeeded in 1991 by Begum Khaleda Zia (the widow of a previous leader, Ziaur Rahman), who ruled as head of the Bangladesh Nationalist Party (BNP) until 1996. In that year, after months of confusion, an election was held in June that brought into power Sheikh Hasina Wajed, the leader of the Awami League and the daughter of Sheikh Mujib, the founding leader of Bangladesh in 1971. The two widows were bitter personal enemies, and their mutual animosity poisoned Bangladeshi politics for most of the 1990s and set back the progress of stable democratic institutions in Bangladesh. In 2001, a new election in which approximately 75 percent of the eligible voters turned out (a figure any democracy would be proud of, and one that includes a high percentage of women) brought Zia back into power in a landslide victory.

Institutions

The formal institutions of democracy in Bangladesh are in place. After the collapse of Ershad's authoritarian government in 1990, Bangladesh experienced three successful elections, in 1991, 1996, and 2001. In both 1996 and 2001, moreover, the government in power lost the election and stepped aside (though in both cases not without a period of resistance). The consistently high percentage of voter turnout in all of the elections –

significantly higher than in the United States – is further testament to the faith in democracy exhibited by the Bangladeshi population. There has also been an effort on the part of the central government in the last few years of the 1990s to democratize local government by opening up formerly appointive positions to election and therefore broadening the participation of groups traditionally excluded from the political process, including women both as voters and candidates. In addition, the two dominant political parties are both well-entrenched in terms both of organization and leadership. The Bangladeshi press is for the most part free to express views with which the government disagrees, and the growing presence of non-governmental organizations in Bangladesh insures both alternative sources of information and opportunities for participating in Bangladeshi civil society that lie outside the boundaries of state control. Citizen groups working on public issues such as gender violence are sprouting up as well.

Conditions

In marked contrast to Pakistan, Bangladesh seems to have successfully graduated from authoritarian to democratic government. With every passing year, the principle of civilian control of the military seems to be more thoroughly embedded in Bangladeshi politics. The fact that military governments have been even more corrupt and incompetent than their civilian counterparts has caused very few members of the electorate to favor return to military rule. Although it is too early to say that a rule of law has taken hold, particularly as violence continues to remain a part of political elections and even political conflicts in general, nevertheless respect for the system of law is widespread. Such respect underlies one of the unique institutions in modern democracies: the use of a caretaker government headed by the most recently retired chief justice of the supreme court to supervise the national electoral process. This innovative solution was a consequence of the wealth of mistrust and the poverty of communication between the two main parties, which had reached the point where the credibility of the elections was in jeopardy. Another advantage the young nation has is the ethnic homogeneity of its population, which is overwhelmingly Bengali. Although the vast majority – approximately 90 percent – of the population is Muslim, there is a minority of Hindus who have in the past remained politically inactive.

Perhaps the greatest immediate impediment to the continued growth of a healthy democracy in Bangladesh is the lack of leadership of both political parties. Sheikh Hasina, the head of the Awami League, and Khaleda Zia, the head of the Bangladesh National Party, seem unable to overcome their personal feud in order to cooperate effectively on issues of national importance. Unfortunately, they have also proven to be very effective at suppressing the rise of new leaders in their respective parties who might be better stewards of the public interest.

The attitudes of the government toward a market economy have shifted with time. The Awami League under Sheik Hasina has tended to endorse the more socialist policies of her father, Sheik Mujib, while the BNP has been more committed to a market economy. The greatest challenge of the future to the economy – apart from downturns in world markets – is environmental. The fact that most of the country is barely above sea level makes it especially vulnerable to crippling floods from overflowing rivers and cyclones blowing in from the Bay of Bengal. In the longer term, if global warming continues to the point that the world's sea level begins to rise, the effect on Bangladesh will be catastrophic.

Sri Lanka
History

Sri Lanka, the beautiful island nation off the southeastern coast of India, is a textbook case in how to undermine democracy from within. Once a beacon of participatory government in the region – having been the first in South Asia to adopt universal adult suffrage in 1931 – Sri Lanka (then known as Ceylon) adopted a fully democratic parliamentary form of government at independence in 1948. For the first decade following independence, the system worked well, until gradually ethnic mistrust between the dominant Sinhalese and the minority Tamils was exploited by self-serving politicians to win elections. In 1983, that smoldering mistrust exploded into a devastating civil war that undermined the foundations of liberal democracy. John Stuart Mill's warnings in the nineteenth century about the dangers to democracy of the tyranny of the majority were never more fully realized than in the history of Sri Lanka in the second half of the twentieth century.

The ethnic makeup in Sri Lanka began to take on its present configuration more than two thousand years ago, when the island was first populated by Indo-Aryans from north India speaking what came to be known as the Sinhala language. When Buddhism arrived from India, the Sinhalese embraced it wholeheartedly and retained it ever since, in spite of its having later died out in India itself. Buddhism remains a powerful social and political force in Sri Lanka to this day. The other main ethnic group is descended from Tamil immigrants who began to migrate there from south India in the third century BC. Their numbers were later augmented by another wave of Tamil immigrants brought in by the British during the nineteenth century to work in the plantations.

Sri Lanka was ruled by independent kingdoms throughout the first millennium and a half of its existence until the arrival of the Portuguese at the beginning of the sixteenth century. After approximately 150 years of Portuguese suzerainty, control of the island passed to the Dutch for another 150 years before the British took over in 1798 and ruled it until independence in 1948. The British influence has been by far the most lasting, leaving its stamp on the language and institutions of the country that endures to the presentday. The British at first resisted Sri Lankan movements for democratic representative government. By the early 1930s, however, they began to create the institutions of elective government that laid the groundwork for independence in 1948.

The first years of the new country were remarkably hopeful. Government changed hands several times in elections that were widely regarded as fair. More than three-quarters of eligible voters turned out to cast their ballots, an extraordinary record for any democracy. In 1960 Sirimavo Bandaranaike, the widow of prime minister S.W.R.D. Bandaranaike (who had been assassinated months earlier) became the first female prime minister in the world. The party she led, known as the Sri Lanka Freedom Party (SLFP) has remained one of the two main parties in Sri Lanka ever since. Its main rival has been the United National Party whose most important leader was J.R. Jayewardene.

Until 1983, democracy flourished. But the seeds of trouble had already been planted in the late 1950s when leading politicians, including both Bandaranaikes and Jayewardene, had caved in to pressure groups – including the influential Buddhist clergy – who were advocating pro-Sinhalese policies that threatened to turn the Tamil minority into second-class citizens. The Tamils, representing approximately 12 percent of the population, became alarmed and began to advocate autonomy for the northern region in which the majority lived. The Sinhalese not only refused this wish, but passed legislation favoring Sinhalese language at the expense of Tamil. The flash point came when Sinhalese mobs killed hundreds of Tamils in the summer of 1983, sparking a civil war that lasted two decades and killed almost 60,000 people. The Tamil side was led by the Liberation Tigers of Eelam (LTTE), who proceeded to assassinate not only Sinhalese but also moderate Tamils who opposed their violent methods. When Indian troops were brought in to suppress them in the 1980s, the LTTE even assassinated the former prime minister of India, Rajiv Gandhi, as well as the president of Sri Lanka.

In 1994, Sirimavo's daughter Chandrika Bandaranaike Kumaratunga, whose own husband had also been assassinated, was elected president (which was now the head of government according to the terms of a new constitution promulgated in 1978) on a platform of ending the war, but was stymied by Sinhalese nationalists and Buddhist clergy. Only in 2003 did circumstances begin to favor a peaceful resolution of the conflict, and negotiations began under the auspices of Norwegian diplomats that brought the parties together with some measure of hope. Democracy, which had been one of the first casualties of the civil war that broke out with vicious ferocity in 1983, finally appeared to be on the mend.

Institutions

The greatest strength of Sri Lankan democracy, as noted above, is its long heritage of elections for more than a half century, many of which have resulted in a change in government. Most of those elections, moreover, were reasonably fair and free. There has existed in Sir Lanka a remarkable tradition of freedom of expression, though that tradition has been compromised in the last two decades by the turbulence of the civil war. Access to information not under the control of the government has been relatively open, due in large part to the proximity of Sri Lanka to India as well as to the widespread English literacy of the educated middle class.

The Achilles' heel of democratic institutions in Sri Lanka has been ethnic or communal conflict. One of the first measures undertaken by politicians in the 1950s eager to pander to Sinhalese nationalists was to disenfranchise the Tamils who had immigrated to Sri Lanka in the last decades of British rule to work on the plantations (augmenting the Tamils who had lived on the island for centuries). The intervening decades of repression and violence resulted in hundreds of thousands of Tamils emigrating either to Europe and the United States or to India, further reducing the ratio of Tamils to Sinhalese in the country and alarming those Tamils who elected to remain in Sri Lanka.

The future success of democracy in Sri Lanka will depend on the ability of the government to create a new institutional structure that will devolve a significant measure of central power to the Tamil communities. The underlying principle must be one of subsidiarity, which holds that the power to make decisions in government should be made at the lowest possible level. Without a much greater degree of local autonomy than ever before, Tamils will continue to believe that their interests will be ignored by the majority Sinhalese.

Conditions

The military in Sri Lanka have remained under the control of civilian elected officials, as they have in India. Credit for this achievement must lie with the heritage of democratic beliefs and political culture that goes back to the 1930s and British willingness to lay the groundwork for parliamentary government. To be sure, it took the British government its own sweet time to arrive at that point, but once it did, it was able to do a creditable job of building a rule of law and a civic culture favoring democracy that endured long after the British departed.

Once independent, the government itself made remarkable progress. It established a system of free education that included both boys and girls. Estimates are that approximately 50 percent of the population in Sri Lanka was literate at independence in 1948. By the 1990s that figure had grown to the low 90s percentile for both men and women, higher by a wide margin than anywhere else in south Asia. Although the government was committed to a socialist ideal of a dominant public sector under the first generation of Bandaranaikes, in the 1980s and 1990s a market system became much more pervasive. One can only hope that over time the widening scope of the middle class in both the Sinhalese and the Tamil communities will eventually lead to more stable and cooperative habits of political interaction. The greatest threat to Sri Lankan democracy in the future, as it has been in the immediate past, is its sub-cultural pluralism. Over the long haul, the simple fact that the Sinhalese and Tamil communities coexisted peacefully for millennia would give grounds for hope that they may once again find a way to heal the wounds created by the populist politicians of the post-independence period.

Overall, the lessons of the Sri Lankan experience are sobering. Democracy can be lost as well as won. It can be frittered away through complacency, and it can be hollowed out and converted into an empty shell through ethnic violence. Without leadership and in the absence of widespread commitment to compromise and tolerance, democracy cannot survive. In Europe in the 1930s, democracies were unable to protect themselves against the ideologies of fear and hatred that grew out of the moral and physical rubble of the First World War and the ensuing depression. In Germany, democracy simply disappeared. In France and Britain, democratic governments lapsed into a paralysis of leadership. In Sri Lanka as well, democracy fell hostage to fear and hatred. When politicians sowed the winds of communal politics, the common people of Sri Lanka reaped the whirlwind. Although the situation there now appears to be on the mend, the lessons of Sri Lanka's experience ought to stand as a tragic warning to contemporary India, where a lesser order of mediocre and populist politicians continue to feed on the ethnic fears of their constituents to win votes.

Conclusion

Given the fact that democratic institutions in South Asia have been relatively more successful over the past half century in India and Sri Lanka than in Muslim Pakistan and Bangladesh, some observers have drawn the conclusion that Islam has played a significant role in suppressing democratic forces in South Asia. Such a view overlooks the importance of the specific economic and social structures of each of these states that are a historical legacy of long standing.[3]

Both Pakistan and Bangladesh had to build their political structures from scratch, whereas India and Sri Lanka inherited well-oiled bureaucratic systems from the British period. Both India and Sri Lanka were led for years after independence by civilian leaders whose political and moral stature were never questioned by their counterparts in the military. There was no landlord class or dominant ethnic group in India, and in Sri Lanka it was not until the late 1950s that communal politics began to raise its ugly head. In Pakistan and Bangladesh, the military was virtually the only effective institution immediately after independence, and was therefore relied upon to take responsibility for tasks that would normally be fulfilled by civilian agencies.

Once having tasted the sweet fruit of power, the army was not inclined to give it up. Although some currents in Islam may have played a role in fostering anti-democratic attitudes – and the cooperation between the military and fundamentalist Islamic groups in Pakistan over the years are certainly evidence in favor of that view – it is clearly less important than these other factors that have bedeviled Pakistan and Bangladesh for so many decades. The challenges for the future have less to do with religious affiliation than with laying the institutional groundwork and fostering the conditions conducive to democratic governance. In doing so the international community can play a vital supportive role in encouraging stable economic growth.

Notes

1 Iftikhar H. Malik, *State and Civil Society in Pakistan* (New York: St. Martin's Press, 1997), p. 259.
2 *Economist* (October 14, 2000).
3 The best short discussion of this topic, from which I have drawn my remarks, is Robin Jeffrey's article entitled 'Democracy in South Asia' in *History Today* (May 1994), pp. 43–47.

Further reading

General

See Richard Charles Crook and James Manor, *Democracy and Decentralisation in South Asia and West Africa: Participation, Accountability, and Performance* (Cambridge: Cambridge University Press, 1998) for a comparative treatment of democratic institutions. For an overall survey of government and politics in Pakistan, Bangladesh, and Sri Lanka (as well as India), see Craig Baxter *et al.*, *Government and Politics in South Asia*, fourth edition (Boulder: Westview Press, 1998). Robert W. Stern, *Democracy and Dictatorship in South Asia: Dominant Classes and Political Outcomes in India, Pakistan, and Bangladesh* (Westport, CT: Praeger, 2001) also has a comparative perspective.

Pakistan

For a collection of studies on democracy in Pakistan see Rasul Bakhsh Rais, ed., *State, Society, and Democratic Change in Pakistan* (Karachi: Oxford University Press, 1997). Judicial issues are covered in Paula R. Newberg, *Judging the State: Courts and Constitutional Politics in Pakistan* (Cambridge: Cambridge University Press, 1993). For a good overview see the chapter on Pakistan in Maya Chadda, *Building Democracy in South Asia: India, Nepal, Pakistan* (Boulder: Lynne Rienner, 2000). For a discussion on the failure of leadership in the early years after Partition see Allen McGrath, *The Destruction of Pakistan's Democracy* (Karachi: Oxford University Press, 1996). Issues of civil society are covered in Iftikhar H. Malik, *State and Civil Society in Pakistan* (New York: St. Martin's Press, 1997). Ayesha Jalal's *Democracy and Authoritarianism in South*

Asia: A Comparative and Historical Perspective (New York: Cambridge University Press, 1995) is useful for comparing the Indian and Pakistani experiences with democracy. *Power and Civil Society in Pakistan*, edited by Anita M. Weiss and S. Zulfiqar Gilani (Karachi: Oxford University Press, 2001), contains papers delivered at a conference on Pakistani civil society at Georgetown University in 1998.

Bangladesh

The scholarly literature on democracy in Bangladesh is unaccountably thin. Two good studies can be found in Shamsul I. Khan, S. Aminul Islam, and M. Indalul Haque, *Political Culture, Political Parties and the Democratic Transition in Bangladesh* (Dhaka: Academic Publisher, 1996); and Kirsten Westergaard, *State and Rural Society in Bangladesh: A Study in Relationship* (London: Curzon, 1985). See also Rehman Sobhan, *Bangladesh: Problems of Governance* (New Delhi: Konark, 1993).

Sri Lanka

S.J. Tambiah's *Sri Lanka: Ethnic Fratricide and the Dismantling of Democracy* (Chicago: University of Chicago Press, 1986) is a standard but now dated source. Sumantra Bose's *States, Nations, Sovereignty: India, Sri Lanka and the Tamil Eelam Movement* (New Delhi: Sage, 1994) is good for background. David Little's *Sri Lanka: The Invention of Enmity* (Washington, DC: United States Institute of Peace Press, 1994) is cautiously optimistic that the ethnic communities in Sri Lanka, who had lived in relative peace for centuries, can ultimately reconcile their differences. See also Lisa M. Kois, Dana Francis, and Robert I. Rotberg, *Sri Lanka's Civil War and Prospects for Post-Conflict Resolution* (Cambridge, MA: World Peace Foundation, 1998). For a discussion of ethnic conflict, consult A. Jeyaratnam Wilson, *Sri Lankan Tamil Nationalism* (Vancouver: University of British Columbia Press, 2000). James Manor, *The Expedient Utopian: Bandaranaike and Ceylon* (Cambridge: Cambridge University Press, 1989) is a good biography. A good collection of studies can be found in Jonathan Spencer, ed., *Sri Lanka: History and the Roots of Conflict* (London and New York: Routledge, 1990).

Chapter 7

Conclusion

This study began with the proposition that democracy is not merely a Western institution but the manifestation of a universal aspiration of the human personality for freedom. Certain aspects of that aspiration are evident even in the early evolution of the human species. For hundreds of thousands if not millions of years, hunter-gatherer societies organized themselves as egalitarian communities with broad participation in decision-making. Equality, in that context, preserved a maximum amount of liberty for the individual by diffusing power to the collective. Hunter-gatherers, in the words of one anthropologist, were 'guided by a love of personal freedom.'[1] The first sedentary and literate society to revive that principle of participatory governance was classical Greece, followed by republican Rome, medieval Italian city-states, and then Britain and the United States. But the number of countries who could reasonably be called democracies in the nineteenth century was very small. By the first half of the twentieth century, even their existence was put at risk by the rise of totalitarian and fascist governments.

For most of the twentieth century, as it turned out, global politics was dominated by a struggle between totalitarian and democratic states. For at least the first three-quarters of the century, totalitarian governments appeared to be winning that struggle. In the 1920s and 1930s, democracies appeared weak and indecisive. Their dithering in the face of growing fascist movements in Europe contributed significantly to the outbreak of the Second World War. By 1949, China had joined the ranks of totalitarian governments, further undermining confidence in the capacity of the world's democracies to escape what appeared to be a rising tide of communism around the world. In the 1960s the United States entered into a long war in Vietnam against a totalitarian adversary and lost. Even as recently as the 1980s the prospects for democracy appeared so dismal that one of the leading intellectuals of Europe, Jean-François Revel, published a sensational study entitled *How Democracies Perish* in which he argued that democracies were doomed because they were incapable of generating the unity of purpose that totalitarian states could. Democracy appeared to be in mortal danger.

By the end of the 1980s, however, two things had changed. First, the Soviet Union collapsed and the Cold War came to an end with a whimper and not a bang. Capitalism and democracy had not only survived; they appeared to have prospered even as their communist and totalitarian adversaries fell on hard times or disappeared altogether. Second, by the 1990s a number of other countries outside the West began to cross the threshold from authoritarian government to genuine democracy. The republics of South Korea and Taiwan were among the most remarkable new members of that club. Meanwhile India, the largest of the non-Western democracies, survived serious threats to popular rule. Suddenly it appeared that democracy was not perishing at all. On the contrary, it was spreading.

The Harvard political scientist Samuel Huntington, as I have noted above, described this phenomenon as the third wave of democratization, though he identified it as starting earlier than I have.[2] According to Huntington, the first wave of democratization occurred in the last few years of the nineteenth century, the second wave after the Second World War, and the third wave after 1974. The first wave was stopped by the rise of totalitarian power, the second by the Cold War. The third continues to gather strength.

The success of these new democracies has given rise to new theories explaining their origin. Whereas the old explanation for democracy had been primarily political (arguing that it derived from the heritage of institutional pluralism rooted in European feudalism), a new explanation now arose that focused on economic factors. According to this new dispensation, the prosperity generated by market capitalism produces a well-educated middle class that over time demands greater political freedom (as it did in England in the second half of the eighteenth century). To be sure, a strong middle class doesn't always lead to democracy. Weimar Germany's advanced economy hadn't protected it from tyranny in 1933. On the other hand (according to the proponents of the economic theory of democracy), Hitler came to power only after the middle class had been undermined by the inflation of the 1920s. So the general lines of the argument still seemed plausible.[3]

In any case, during the hopeful atmosphere of the 1990s, the economic argument seemed to carry the day. It still does, for reasons that are perfectly justifiable. Capitalism did indeed play a vital role in fostering democratic institutions, as did the political pluralism generated by the feudal regimes in Western Europe in the Middle Ages. The aim of this particular study of the Asian experience with democracy is not to argue in favor of one or the other of these theories but rather to show, through a diversity of specific examples, how richly complex the actual experience of Asian democracy has been. As important as economic and political forces have been, they have also interacted with social, historical, cultural, and very personal and purely contingent influences to create a dynamic mix of circumstance that is unique to each country. What is endlessly fascinating to me as an observer and writer of history is the always shifting relationship between a universal typology of an institution such as democracy and the particular experience of any given country. Perhaps one of the outcomes of this study might be to make us all more comfortable with ambiguity when we use terms like democracy in our everyday conversations. There may be many paths to the same goal of democracy, as there may be many forms of democracy. None of them is perfect, all have strengths and weaknesses, and each has much to learn from the experience of the others.

With that caveat in mind, I also want to make a stab at identifying some common themes that emerge naturally from the experiences chronicled in these pages. The first harkens back to the complementary relationship between freedom and authority outlined in the preface to this book. Over and over again we have seen democratic institutions rise out of social and political traditions that place considerable emphasis on authority. For that matter, we have also seen examples of democratic states in Asia that have slipped back into authoritarian regimes for one reason or another. What I hope has been gained is a greater appreciation for the value of a reasonable balance between these two attributes of political life. To see them exclusively as antithetical is to underestimate their potential for positive interaction. In many cases in Asia, authoritarian regimes actually laid the institutional foundations for the subsequent rise of democracy. Asian democracy may have antecedents that are different from those of the West, but that does not mean that the desire for freedom among the peoples of Asia is any less strong.

Another theme is the courage of students in so many countries of Asia. Their willingness to shed blood in the streets demonstrating against repressive policies of autocratic rulers has frequently been the catalyst for change that resulted in the overthrow of the old regime and the adoption of a more democratic system. Yes, students may not understand the nuances of democratic theory or practice, and yes, demonstrating in the streets is only one way of bringing about public participation. In some cases, public confrontation provoked by students can even make matters worse, as happened in China after the Tiananmen Square crackdown in June 1989. Nevertheless, from South Korea to Thailand to Indonesia, students have been a significant force for change. Idealism and courage *can* change the world.

A third theme is the importance of leadership. Over and over again, in almost every country covered by this study, leadership has tipped the balance either in favor of democracy or against it. Jawaharlal Nehru's legacy in India is perhaps the best example of the crucial role of integrity in nurturing the healthy growth of democratic institutions. In our own day we also have a dramatic example of the same phenomenon. No one can travel to South Africa or review its modern history without marveling at the extraordinary impact wielded by leaders like Nelson Mandela and Desmond Tutu through the example of their moral authority. That they lived most of their adult life in a society manifestly unjust and brutally destructive of basic human dignity, without losing their humanity, is already remarkable enough. But then to go so far beyond that, to emerge out of this cauldron of evil and call upon their followers to treat their former tormentors with forgiveness and reconciliation, is one of the great achievements of human history.

On the other hand, in other cases such as in the Philippines under Marcos and Sri Lanka under the Bandaranaikes, poor leadership has shut down democracy and moved it toward dictatorship or chaos. These examples are sobering reminders that democracy is not, by itself, a perfect system. However many safeguards are built into the structure to prevent abuse, the fact is that every democracy is led by fallible human beings elected by equally fallible voters, all of whom make errors of judgment. Under the stress of poverty, ignorance, war, or a multitude of other potential threats, the likelihood that people will commit tragic errors of judgment multiplies. Democracy, as Churchill so famously pointed out, is the worst form of government, except for all the others. Failure to understand this basic reality, and failure to teach it in the school system, will lead inevitably to such a degree of complacency that the whole enterprise of democracy may be put in jeopardy. Presumably that is what the American abolitionist Wendell Phillips had in mind when he noted that eternal vigilance is the price of liberty.

A fourth theme is subsidiarity, the doctrine that decisions in a government (or in any organization) ought to be made at the lowest possible level. In all cases covered by this study, governments that were highly centralized were more ineffective, and less democratic, than those who had devolved power from the center to the periphery. This theme may appear to border on a tautology, since one might well argue that democracy, by definition, embodies the principle of public participation, which in turn implies a spreading out of power to the lowest possible levels. But it is worth stressing simply because there is a tendency in any organization to centralize decision-making, forgetting that such a policy may be efficient but not necessarily effective. The confusion between the two is often the cause of much distress at the level of implementation.

A fifth theme is the importance of institutional and ideological pre-requisites for democracy. Robert Putnam's famous study of the different attitudes toward democracy among communities in Italy is instructive here.[4] He found that in northern Italy there was a long tradition of local civic organizations who owe their existence not to government but to habits of cooperation and association extending centuries into the past. In southern Italy, by contrast, organizations historically are not formed from the bottom up but from the top down, a consequence of a patron–client social structure that stifles civic participation. Not surprisingly, democracy fares much better in the horizontally based society of the north than the vertically based society of the south. By following the practice of subsidiarity, northerners encourage an active, participatory civic life, while southerners tend to wait passively for someone else to step in and take care of them. In Putnam's view, the disparity between the wealthy north and the poor south is in large part a consequence of this difference in their civic institutions. Not surprisingly, those governments in Asia that have fostered subsidiarity have tended to build stronger foundations for democratic rule.

Overall, should one be optimistic or pessimistic about the prospects for democracy in Asia? My answer is both. There is plenty of evidence for pessimism. Robert Dahl has noted that in the twentieth century 'on more than seventy occasions democracy collapsed and gave way to an authoritarian regime.'[5] Capitalism may encourage democracy by fostering pluralistic institutions, but it also simultaneously discourages democracy by fostering inequality. Money corrupts politics just as it corrupts individuals. Democracy and capitalism both reinforce each other and undermine each other at the same time. There will always be tension between the two, as well as partnership. We are also well advised to beware of the tyranny of the majority, particularly during times of ethnic conflict or fear. Justice Brandeis once wrote that 'fear breeds repression; repression breeds hate; that hate menaces stable government.'[6] Democracies are no exception to that rule. By the same token, one of the pillars of democracy – a free press – can become so corrupted by money that it no longer is able to play its natural role as a critic of government. It can become merely an adjunct of larger corporate empires whose commitment to truth is often overshadowed by their search for profits. In the United States, the gradual slide of the fourth estate into the pockets of the entertainment industry (which seeks to curry favor with politicians) is perhaps one of the most pernicious examples of the manner in which a functioning democracy can become corrupted. Democracy can decline, as can all other forms of government.

But there is much evidence for optimism as well. If one is willing to take into account the vastly different historical and institutional heritage of Asian countries, and appreciate the direction of underlying trends that may be invisible to outsiders, then there are many hopeful signs. Technology may also favor democracy, in contrast to George Orwell's fears in *1984*. During the student demonstrations in Tiananmen Square in the spring of 1989, one of the most effective forms of communication among students groups in China was faxing messages to friends in the United States, who would then re-fax them to other students in China. Some wit referred to this phenomenon as the 'fax Americana.' Today, of course, the role of the fax machine has been supplanted by the Internet, which has vastly increased the amount of information not controlled by the government available to the public. One can only assume that the less control a given government has over the information available to its citizens, the greater the opportunity for freedom of thought.

Overall, I am optimistic because I believe so deeply in the universality of the human impulse to be free. I am willing to concede that the price of giving people the freedom to choose between right and wrong is that many will make the wrong choice. That is precisely what Dostoevsky was grappling with in the famous Grand Inquisitor chapter of the *Brothers Karamazov*. In that profound passage Christ was reputed to have returned to earth during the Spanish Inquisition, and was arrested for disturbing the peace. The Grand Inquisitor visited him in prison and accused him of having made a mistake in bestowing upon humankind the gift of freedom. No sooner did people have that freedom, the Grand Inquisitor claimed, than they abused it by choosing evil over good. The job of the Church, therefore, was to rectify that error by forcing people to do what is good through whatever means necessary, including burning them at the stake. (The twentieth-century version of this, of course, were the Marxist-Leninist and fascist states who killed tens of millions of people in the name of human progress.) In Dostoevsky's novel, Christ's response is to listen in silence to the Inquisitor's monologue, and then respond with a kiss, to answer his argument, in effect, with love.

In the end, democracy is the best form of government because it takes into account this fundamentally human inclination to do both what is right, and what is wrong. That paradox is unavoidable, an inevitable consequence of human freedom. The great Protestant theologian Reinhold Niebuhr, mindful of this potential for both good and evil in the human personality, once remarked that 'man's capacity for justice makes democracy possible; but man's inclination to injustice makes democracy necessary.'[7] We would do well to remember that insight not only as we evaluate the young democracies of Asia, but also the 'mature' democracies in the West.

So if we can agree that democracy's gift to humankind is freedom, the final question is: freedom to do what? Are we endowed with the gift of freedom simply to gratify our own pleasures? To seek individual happiness? Do we have freedom only to become slaves to our passions? Perhaps it is appropriate to end our discussion with these questions, since they transcend the subject of this book. Asking them, however, underscores the simple and important truth that democracy is a tool, an institutional means to a moral and spiritual end. It is not an end in itself. Whether we use this tool for good or for evil depends on the choices that you and I make every day of our lives. Democracy, in the end, is just the beginning.

Notes

1 So said the anthropologist Christopher Boehm in *Hierarchy in the Forest: The Evolution of Egalitarian Behavior* (Cambridge, MA: Harvard University Press, 1999), p. 65.

2 Samuel P. Huntington, *The Third Wave: Democratization in the Late Twentieth Century* (Norman: University of Oklahoma Press, 1991).

3 For the record, there are many scholars who disagree with this proposition, among the most lucid of whom is Fareed Zakaria, *The Future of Freedom: Illiberal Democracy at Home and Abroad* (New York: W.W. Norton, 2003).

4 *Making Democracy Work: Civic Traditions in Modern Italy* (Princeton: Princeton University Press, 1993).
5 Robert Dahl, *On Democracy* (New Haven: Yale University Press, 1998), p. 145.
6 *Whitney* v. *California*, 274 U.S. 357, 375–377 (1927).
7 Reinhold Niebuhr, *The Children of Light and the Children of Darkness* (New York: Scribners, 1944), p. xiii.

Further reading

For a clearly written and critical appraisal of democracy, focused primarily on the United States, see Benjamin R. Barber, *A Place for Us: How to Make Society Civil and Democracy Strong* (New York: Hill and Wang, 1998). For a discussion of the connection between standards of behavior and democracy (in America), see Stephen Carter, *Civility: Manners, Morals, and the Etiquette of Democracy* (New York: Basic Books, 1998). Anything by Larry Diamond on democracy is worth reading. See particularly three books edited by Diamond and others: Larry Diamond and Marc F. Plattner, eds, *The Global Resurgence of Democracy*, second edition (Baltimore: Johns Hopkins University Press, 1996); Larry Diamond, Juan J. Linz, Seymour Martin Lipset, eds, *Politics in Developing Countries: Comparing Experiences with Democracy*, second edition (Boulder: Lynne Rienner, 1995); and Larry Diamond and Marc F. Plattner, *Economic Reform and Democracy* (Baltimore: Johns Hopkins University Press, 1995). For an excellent collection of readings on Western democracy, see Philip Green, *Democracy* (Atlantic Highlands, New Jersey: Humanities Press, 1993). David Held's *Democracy and the Global Order: From the Modern State to Cosmopolitan Governance* (Stanford: Stanford University Press, 1995) is a fine discussion of democratic theory and a global world. Samuel P. Huntington's *The Third Wave: Democratization in the Late Twentieth Century* (Norman: University of Oklahoma Press, 1991) was a highly influential work. Jean Francois Revel's *How Democracies Perish* (New York: Doubleday, 1984) created a sensation when its English translation appeared. Lars Rudebeck and Olle Törnquist's edited volume *Democratization in the Third World: Concrete Cases in Comparative and Theoretical Perspective* (New York: St. Martin's Press, 1998) contains some interesting studies, as does the edited volume by Geraint Parry and Michael Moran, *Democracy and Democratization* (New York: Routledge, 1994). Robert K. Schaeffer's *Power to the People: Democratization Around the World* (Boulder: Westview Press, 1997) is a good survey of democratic conditions on a global scale.

Index

101, 102; Sri Lanka Freedom Party
(SLFP) 100; suffrage 99, 100;
Tamil uprising 36; United National
Party 100; women 101
Stoicism 8–10
student demonstrations 107; China
64, 65–66, 109; Indonesia 86–87;
South Korea 56; Thailand 73
subsidiarity 108–109; Bangladesh 98;
China 63, 66; India 13; Indonesia
87; Sri Lanka 101; Thailand 74
suffrage 2, 7, 11; Britain 3, 28; India
36, 38; Japan 41; Philippines 46;
Sri Lanka 99, 100; Thailand 72;
United States of America 2–3, 29;
see also elections
Suharto 86, 87, 88, 89
Sukarno 86, 87, 89
Sulla, Lucius Cornelius 12
Switzerland 14

Taiwan: access to information 59, 60;
broadcast media 60, 61; and China
58, 60–61, 62, 67–68; citizenship
60; conditions for democracy
60–61; Confucianism 68–69;
corruption 60; democracy 52, 53,
59; Democratic Progressive Party
(DPP) 59, 61; economy 52, 58, 59,
61; elections 55, 58, 59; ethnic
conflict 59, 61; freedom to associate
60; history 57–59; institutions
59–60; Japanese occupation 58;
Kuomintang Party (KMT) 58, 59,
60, 61; language 61; military 60;
police 60; print media 59
taxation 8, 28
Thailand: access to information 75;
Assembly of the Poor 76;
Association of Rural Doctors 76;
broadcast media 75; bureaucracy
74; Chinese population 77;
conditions for democracy 75–78;

constitutional monarchy 72, 73–74;
constitutional reforms 73, 74, 75;
corruption 73, 74, 77; democracy
73, 74; economy 76, 77; education
77; elections 73, 74, 75; ethnic
diversity 77; history 72–73;
inequalities 77; institutions 73–75,
77; labor unions 75; local
government 74; middle class 76,
77; military 72, 73, 74, 75, 76;
monarchy 72; non-governmental
organizations (NGOs) 76;
patron–client relationships 74;
police 75; political parties 73, 79;
print media 75; sovereignty 72;
student demonstrations 73; suffrage
72; Thai Communist Party 76
Thaksin Shinawatra 74, 77
Thucydides 6, 22 (n2)
Tocqueville, Alexis de 6, 30
totalitarianism 64, 105, 106
Tunku Abdul Rahman 79
Tutu, Desmond 107–108

United States of America: in
Afghanistan 95, 96; Cold War 13;
cultural homogeneity 15;
democracy 28–29; education 69;
factionalism 12; foreign
intervention by 13; global power
15–16; in Japan 41, 44; justice 14;
Korean War 55; in Philippines 45,
47; press 109; public morality 6–7;
public office 29; republic 29;
Second World War 15, 41; slavery
9, 28; suffrage 2–3, 29; taxation 8;
two-party system 14; Vietnam War
105

Vietnam xi, 72, 76, 105

Wahid, Abdurrahman 87
war x, 15; civil wars 58, 64, 99, 100;